The Untapped Power of the Sacrament of Penance

THE UNTAPPED POWER
OF THE SACRAMENT
OF PENANCE

A Priest's View

Father Christopher J. Walsh

PUBLISHED BY ST. ANTHONY MESSENGER PRESS
CINCINNATI, OHIO

Excerpts from Scripture passages have been taken from *New Revised Standard Version Bible,* copyright ©1989 by the Division of Christian Education of the National Council of the Churches of Christ in the U.S.A., and used by permission. All rights reserved.

Personal stories in this book have been used by permission. Names and/or some details have been changed to protect the privacy of the contributors.

Cover design by Candle Light Studios
Book design by Phillips Robinette, O.F.M.

Library of Congress Cataloging-in-Publication Data

Walsh, Christopher J. (Christopher James)
  The untapped power of the Sacrament of penance / Christopher J. Walsh.
    p. cm.
  Includes index.
  ISBN 0-86716-658-4 (pbk. : alk. paper) 1. Penance—Catholic Church. 2. Confession—Catholic Church. 3. Reconciliation—Religious aspects—Christianity. I. Title.

BX2260.W34 2005
234'.166—dc22
                        2005009934

ISBN 0-86716-658-4

Published by Servant Books, an imprint of St. Anthony Messenger Press
28 W. Liberty St.
Cincinnati, OH 45202
www.AmericanCatholic.org

Printed in the United States of America

Printed on acid-free paper

05 06 07 08 09 5 4 3 2 1

To my parents

Contents

Foreword

Father Christopher Walsh, a friend of mine for many years, has written this stimulating and engaging discussion of something that needed to be said emphatically to Catholics of our time. Any reasonably literate and serious Catholic will enjoy reading these pages about the sacrament of reconciliation, which unfortunately has tended to fall by the wayside in the confusion of the post-Vatican II era. Like a number of other elements in Catholic life, it is now beginning to make a comeback, and this book should be an important contribution to this blessing for the church.

We might ask why the sacrament of reconciliation, or confession, dropped out of Catholic life. It was so eminently important, even in the early 1960s. To my way of thinking there were several reasons.

The first is that people went to confession too often. Large numbers of people went every week or at least every two weeks. Parishes had four or five priests hearing confessions for four hours every Saturday. Actually, a large number of those confessions contained little or nothing of a really sinful nature. They could have been taken care of by a good act of contrition.

Many times I had people confess to me that they did not kneel down when they said their morning prayers or they forgot to say grace before lunch one day. Often I had to ask people to mention a sin from the past so that I could give them valid absolution. Some priests compared this experience to being pecked to death by ducks. I sometimes tell seminarians that the reason confessionals were built with small windows was to keep the priest from jumping out of them.

Another reason for the decline in confessions is the reduced number of priests. With today's increased Catholic population and the smaller number of priests, we could not possibly hear the number of weekly or bimonthly confessions that priests did in the past.

Perhaps the most important reason for the decline is that, in order to handle the needs of many penitents, priests were restricted to giving a couple of pious words of encouragement. Seminarians were given the goal of completing each person's confession in two minutes or fewer. This was a rather mechanical approach to the sacrament and may not have contributed much to the purpose of reconciliation, which is repentance.

Father Walsh takes on all the traditional questions that people ask about confession, including why we go to confession to a man and not directly to Christ. He gives fresh and engaging answers, which informed Catholics should review. When older Catholics read the chapter headings, they may be inclined to say, "I know that answer." Read Father Walsh's answer and the discussion, and you will come away with some new ideas.

I found that the most engaging part of the book was the discussion of three aspects of this sacrament that, although of equal importance, may not always be seen that way. These aspects are healing, forgiveness and reconciliation.

The healing, or therapeutic, model calls on the priest to be a healer of souls. I have to confess that this is the model I have operated on for most of my priesthood. Without ignoring the other two purposes of the sacrament of reconciliation, I find the healing aspect to be the most meaningful for me, possibly because I am a psychologist. Even though I play down that role in comparison with the priesthood, I approach such things at least partially from the viewpoint of that profession. And it seems as if the therapeutic model is both effective and popular at the present time.

Father Walsh also outlines the judicial model. The priest fulfills the role of judge in exercising the power, conferred by Christ, to loose or bind sins.

Finally, there is the relational model of the sacrament. Confession brings sinners back to God and helps them regain, if they have lost it, their place in the body of Christ. This model, of course, is based on the image of the Good Shepherd, who seeks the lost sheep, and ultimately on the merciful God, whom we meet in both the Old and New Testament.

These three models are complementary, and I suppose you can evaluate the effectiveness of the sacrament at the present time from whichever model you prefer. While it is true that there is a tremendous decline in the number of people who come to receive the sacrament of reconciliation, nonetheless many are in need of it because of the state of their soul. There is no doubt that those who do come are usually looking for spiritual healing and strengthening, as well as sacramental absolution.

For years my main experience with hearing confessions has been at St. Patrick's Cathedral, where the friars help out once a week. I have often told fellow priests that you will always hear the best confessions at St. Patrick's Cathedral. People are well prepared, know how to confess and honestly ask for help.

I should point out that many of those who come to the cathedral for confession are fairly recent immigrants to the United Sates—from the Orient, the Philippines, Africa, the Caribbean or Latin America. They generally appear to be well instructed and make good and solid confessions. People whose confessions seem superficial or marked by a good deal of confusion are often the products of religious education in the United States in the last quarter century.

St. Patrick's is a wonderful place to hear confessions because I am likely to encounter everybody. It's the only place I've ever had Jewish people come to confess. Obviously they cannot receive the sacrament; in fact, they will tell me they cannot receive absolution but that they need a blessing—a *baruka*, as they say in Hebrew. Occasionally we get a Protestant Christian who feels the need for encouragement.

The therapeutic approach to confession emphasizes the care of souls, although the other aspects are of equal importance. The penitent must surrender to God, admit shortcomings and sins, ask forgiveness and be reconciled. These are beautiful steps in the meaning of confession.

Father Walsh's approach to the sacrament is both traditional and contemporary. He takes on the age-old issues in light of our times. One of the most interesting and moving parts of this book is the description of Father Vincent Capodanno, a priest from Staten Island, New York, who was killed while serving as a military chaplain during the war in

Vietnam. Father Capodanno regularly volunteered to walk into battle areas and give the sacraments to personnel who had been wounded or were dying. In an engagement that Father Walsh describes very powerfully, Father Capodanno knowingly laid down his life to hear confessions and assist the dying while he himself was dying of wounds. This account alone makes the reading of the book worthwhile.

Along with the author, I hope that confession will become frequent again among Catholics—although perhaps not as frequent as it was before the Council, when people often went to confession out of habit. That's good for some people but not for everyone. On the other hand, going to confession on a yearly basis is not helpful at all.

Both laity and clergy need to be encouraged about the sacrament of reconciliation. The sacrament will succeed in a parish and will become popular if it is preached from the pulpit and taught in the school. Then people will come. I pray that Father Walsh's book will herald the end of the logjam that presently surrounds the sacrament of reconciliation.

—Father Benedict J. Groeschel, C.F.R.

CHAPTER ONE

Whatever Happened to the
Sacrament of Penance?

Mario's Place is a well-known spot in Westport, Connecticut. Located across from the train station, it has been a favorite restaurant in town for decades. On weekday evenings New York commuters and local businessmen crowd into the bar for a drink.

Mario, the owner, is a warm, gracious person who is easy to talk to. He loves to tell people how God chose to pour out his saving, reconciling grace on him right in his restaurant. It came through a priest. And it happened in the sacrament of penance.

Mario was raised a Catholic. But ever since his wife died, some ten years before, he hadn't been in church. In fact, he had gotten to the point where he was ashamed to walk into the church after being away from the practice of the faith for so long.

But God was at work in Mario. One afternoon he was sitting by himself at the end of the bar when Father Frank McGrath, the local pastor, walked in. Father came over and sat down with him in the empty taproom, and the two men began chatting. Mario recognized he had an opportunity for more than small talk, and he decided to tell his friend about his situation. Finally he asked, "How can I start coming back to church?"

"You should go to confession," Father Frank replied.

"How do I do that?" Mario continued.

"We can do it right here!" the pastor told him. Mario was dumbfounded.

The two men walked over to a corner table in the empty dining room. Mario confessed his sins, and the priest gave him absolution. Now Mario goes to Mass at Father Frank's church every Saturday evening, where he enjoys sitting up front in one of the first pews.

How Things Have Changed

Whatever happened to the sacrament of penance? Drop in at most Catholic churches on a Saturday afternoon these days, and you may find a handful of people waiting to see the lone priest hearing confessions before the evening liturgy. In some places the priest does not even bother going into the confessional or reconciliation room, unless he sees a penitent enter the church. Sticking his head out of the sacristy from time to time to check, he occupies himself with preparing for the Mass instead.

In other parishes the priests appear to have given up altogether on the sacrament of penance. A line in the bulletin or on the sign in front of the church may read: "Confessions by appointment. Please call the rectory." I would be willing to bet that the parish secretary is not overwhelmed by phone calls to schedule appointments with the priests!

This is a far cry from the scene that would have been encountered in even a mid-sized Catholic parish fifty or sixty years ago. Then several priests would sit for three to four hours on Saturday afternoons and evenings in their respective confessionals, with their nameplates conveniently posted on the door (plus one reserved for the ubiquitous "Father Visitor"). A steady stream of parishioners would slip into the church, kneel briefly for their examination of conscience and then join the slowly shuffling line outside their favorite confessor's box.

The small light above the box would turn from red to green, and the next penitent would slip into that still, dark space behind the confessional door. After a few minutes the grille door would slide open, and a dim light would reveal the silhouette of a priest. His quiet voice would begin the ritual: "In the name of the Father and of the Son and of the Holy Spirit. Amen." And the penitent would respond: "Bless me, Father, for I have sinned. It has been a week since my last confession. These are my sins...."

A retired priest, who as a Columban missioner visited hundreds of churches throughout the northeastern United States from 1945 to 1958, recalls that the norm in many parishes was for all the priests in the rectory, plus visiting priests, to devote themselves to the sacrament of penance on Saturday afternoons from 4:00 to 6:00 P.M., take a break for dinner and then return for evening confessions from 7:30 to 9:00. In addition, most Fridays were devoted to hearing the confessions of all the children in the parish school, which in some cases meant over a thousand students, from second graders to seniors in high school. Suffice it to say that administering the sacrament of penance constituted a significant part of the ministry of a Catholic priest in the years immediately before Vatican II.

The goal of today's church with regard to the sacrament of penance should not be that of resuscitating the 1950s Catholic experience of going to confession. There were undeniably problems in that pastoral practice: a mechanical repetitiveness in confessing sins, a tendency for at least some Catholics to fall into an obsessive preoccupation with guilt and little emphasis by priest or penitent on pursuing a deeper moral discernment and lasting spiritual transformation. Besides, the truth is that in the church's history no sacrament has undergone more radical changes in practice and theology than the sacrament of penance. The developments in liturgical ritual and in pastoral approaches to confession that have occurred since Vatican II are all part of that historical process and on balance are largely positive.

In my judgment, then, the current pastoral crisis regarding the sacrament of penance does not involve a debate over how to celebrate the sacrament but rather the more fundamental concern that the sacrament be celebrated by Catholics integrally, meaningfully and regularly. What we need to consider at the present moment is why the sacrament is so vital and enriching to the Christian life, why many Catholics today appear not to appreciate this and what can be done to remedy the situation. Such is the project for this book.

A Remarkable Gift

I need to say a personal word at the outset, lest this book's title give the impression that the author claims to possess a peculiar competence in the area of confession. I write this book as a simple diocesan priest who marvels at the mercy of God, a God who is willing to use weak, sinful men as his instruments in forgiving sins and reconciling human beings to himself—a power that properly belongs to him alone. I write as a confessor who tries to remember each time he is about to celebrate the sacrament the prayer that I heard a cardinal say that he prays each time he enters the confessional:

"Lord, take me over completely. Let me say only what you would say; let me do only what you would do. Let me not get in the way. Make my priesthood your priesthood."

I also write as a sinful Christian penitent. I myself depend on this wonderful sacrament in order to fight my human weaknesses and moral failings, to seek spiritual counsel amid the challenges of life and to experience the mercy and healing of God in my own soul.

If I have perhaps one particular insight to share, it stems from the fact that for the last thirteen years I have been involved in forming young men to be priests, pastors "according to the heart of Christ." In the various roles of seminary spiritual director, theology professor and diocesan vocation director, I have been drawn to reflect more deeply on the mystery of the sacramental life that priests mediate and that seminarians strive to grasp and appreciate. One conclusion that I have reached is that the sacrament of penance is an absolutely remarkable gift of divine mercy and grace.

The sacramental form of penance is uniquely personal and relational, capable of being adapted to church confessionals or hospital bedsides, prison cells or open battlefields, even chance encounters in restaurants or on the street. The sacrament addresses the spiritual needs of both the repentant criminal and the saint, of the anonymous penitent in need of forgiveness and the devout parishioner seeking regular spiritual guidance and growth. It is traditionally called (along with baptism) a "sacrament of the dead," since even a person who is not in the state of sanctifying grace can receive it, yet the most frequent recipients are practicing Catholics who want to grow in the grace that they already possess. Penance is the most private of sacraments, the most dialogical and the one where the priest has the most freedom and responsibility in deciding what to say and how to shape the recipient's experience. As I will argue in this book, I believe penance is *the* sacrament for contemporary Catholics!

Are there any signs that believers today are coming to appreciate once more these unique benefits of the sacrament of penance? I believe there are.

Two priests from a new Franciscan religious community came to give a retreat in a parish where Saturday afternoon confessions barely filled the hour allotted them. During Lent the parish priests would advertise two town-wide penance services, but only a few parishioners ever attended these. The priests had concluded that their parishioners simply had no great interest in receiving the sacrament of penance.

The two Franciscans, however, wanted to try a different approach. With the support of the new pastor, who had invited them, they actively encouraged parishioners to receive the sacrament, and then they took turns being in the church to hear confessions all day long for the entire week. Word of this passed throughout the parish, and by the end of the retreat, the priests estimated that almost two hundred people had slipped into the church during the day or evening to receive the sacrament of penance. A year later the parish was having confessions for two hours or more every Saturday afternoon.

The Gift of Easter Night

If contemporary Catholics are going to return to the sacrament of penance, they need to rediscover the mystery and power of this incredible gift the risen Lord Jesus bestowed on his church. And they can only rediscover it if they personally experience it, if they themselves encounter the peace and strength of the Holy Spirit as the disciples did in the Upper Room that first Easter Sunday night.

As described in John's dramatic account, Jesus suddenly appears in the midst of the dispirited band of his followers. The apostles are paralyzed by guilt, fear and dejection. "Peace be with you!" Jesus says to them. And immediately he breathes on them and says: "Receive the Holy Spirit. If you forgive the sins of any, they are forgiven them; if you retain the sins of any, they are retained" (John 20:22–23).

The Catholic church sees this event in the Upper Room as the moment of Christ's institution of the sacrament of penance. His very first deed as risen Lord is to bequeath to his church the power to forgive sin. In this way Christ ensures that his apostles and successors will now continue his own messianic mission—freeing human beings from the bonds of sin and death and reconciling them to the Father. "As the Father has sent me, so I send you" (John 20:21).

The Lord's commissioning and sending of the eleven is much more than simply a master's exhortation to his followers to continue teaching his message and imitating his way of life (though it certainly includes this). Jesus is sending the apostles forth with a new identity and power. They and their successors will henceforth exercise that very same power of the Holy Spirit that Jesus exercised. They will speak with that same incredible, unheard of authority that so amazed and scandalized the hearers of Jesus when he said to the paralytic: "Son, your sins are forgiven.... Stand up, take your mat and go to your home" (Mark 2:5, 11). And thus, those whom they touch—especially in those privileged, divinely guaranteed encounters with the grace of Christ called sacraments—will experience the same gift of the Risen One that the apostles themselves received on that first Easter Sunday night: "Peace be with you! Receive the Holy Spirit."

In the church's liturgy in the weeks following Easter, the lectionary presents for our reflection at Mass on two successive days the words of Jesus to Nicodemus: "The wind blows where it chooses, and you hear the sound of it, but you do not know where it comes from or where it goes. So it is with everyone who is born of the Spirit" (John 3:8). As Scripture scholars have long pointed out, there is a wonderful play on words going on in this passage. The Greek word for "wind"—*pneuma*—is also the word for "spirit." John is telling us that the Holy Spirit is a mysterious, powerful, unpredictable force.

Like a tropical storm wind, the Holy Spirit works in a way that is invisible to the eye and unfathomable to the mind trying to predict its movements. We can see the mighty transformations the Spirit of Christ has wrought in the lives of those who believe, but "you do not know where it comes from or where it goes." It is this powerful, transforming grace that is available to all who approach the sacrament of penance.

What concrete steps can the church take today to help Catholics experience the power of Christ's Spirit in the sacrament of penance? Thankfully, some pastoral strategies in the years since Vatican II have worked.

Special retreats and spiritual programs have successfully reintroduced many Catholics to the healing power of confession. One thinks of Cursillos, Marriage and Engaged Encounter and "healing Masses" sponsored by the charismatic renewal; all sorts of programs designed for people dealing with specific addictions or traumas, such as AA retreats for recovering alcoholics and Rachel's Vineyard weekends for victims of abortion; local teen retreat programs such as

Search, Emmaus and Life Teen, plus the national conferences for youth and young adults organized by Franciscan University of Steubenville or the National Catholic Youth Conference.

Confessions are often a key spiritual component of pilgrimages, whether these are day trips to regional shrines and basilicas; never-to-be-forgotten visits to Lourdes, Rome or Medjugorje; or those explosive biennial gatherings of hundreds of thousands—even millions—of young Catholics inaugurated by Pope John Paul II called World Youth Days.

Sometimes all it takes to bring Catholics back to the sacrament of penance is for a pastor to begin preaching about its importance and expanding the times when confessions are offered. Or as we saw in the story just recounted, a priest leading a parish mission can emphasize making a good confession as a key part of its spiritual exercises. Sometimes all that is needed is for a priest to be available when a soul that has been carrying a huge weight of guilt and remorse for years suddenly finds itself "pushed" to receive the sacrament of penance.

The Importance of Hope

There is one other sobering lesson that we learn from the apostles' first encounter with the risen Lord on Easter Sunday night. Only ten of the Twelve were in the Upper Room to receive Christ's forgiveness of their sins of abandonment and denial. Judas despaired that God's Spirit was powerful enough to forgive him, who had betrayed the Lord for thirty pieces of silver. He refused to let the Spirit bring him to conversion and repentance, and so he died in his despair.

Thomas, too, was absent when the Lord appeared to the other apostles that first night of the week. When they recounted to him the incredible event, he refused to believe that the Spirit of God could have raised Jesus from the dead and that Christ would really return to them offering his peace. When Jesus finally meets Thomas a week later, he says to him simply: "Do not doubt but believe" (John 20:27).

The one trait that is forbidden to Christ's followers is despair: to doubt that Jesus Christ truly seeks to save and heal us. Pastoral strategies will not bring people back to the sacrament of penance unless they foster in Christian hearts true hope in the power and love of God. As Pope John Paul II did not cease repeating, we who live at the beginning of the third Christian millennium must not be afraid to "cross the threshold of hope."[1]

For me, the greatest legacy and most inspiring trait of Pope John Paul II was this confident, evangelical, unshakable hope. His faith and hope in the power of Christ's Spirit active in the church did not change from what they were in 1969 when he was archbishop of Krakow. In those difficult years immediately following the Second Vatican Council, Cardinal Wojtyla wrote a letter to his friend, the French Jesuit theologian and Vatican II *peritus* (theological consultant) Henri de Lubac. Sharing de Lubac's profound disappointment at the distortions of the Council's teaching that were being disseminated and suffering like him from the "great crisis" shaking the church, he nevertheless concluded, "We have firmly hoped, we will always hope and we are and will be happy."[2]

As we witnessed the twilight years of his pontificate, many observers of the church and the world still found more shadows than lights, more grounds for despair than for hope. Even the signature program of Pope John Paul II—what since 1983 he heralded as the "new evangelization"—seemed in large parts of the church to have fallen on deaf ears and at least for the present to have met with very mixed results. Yet in his writings and in his pastoral activity John Paul's message did not change.

And despite his severely limited physical capacity in his final years, he seemed no less committed to the conviction that he proclaimed with such inspiring zeal in his 1990 encyclical *Redemptoris Missio* ("The Mission of the Redeemer"): "God is opening before the Church the horizons of a humanity more fully prepared for the sowing of the Gospel. I sense that the moment has come to commit all of the Church's energies to a new evangelization and to the mission *ad gentes.* No believer in Christ, no institution of the Church, can avoid this supreme duty: to proclaim Christ to all peoples."[3]

Did Pope John Paul see something that church commentators and theological experts do not? Is there a movement of the Spirit going on below the radar screen of negative news and gloomy statistics and alarmist predictions (such as, "In fifty years there will be no more priests!"), which goes undetected but is real?

I believe the answer is yes. Not that we are living in an age when it is easy to be optimistic. But perhaps for that very reason, precisely because of the loss of confidence in all the ideologies that have propelled the spirit of the modern world for the last two hundred years—scientism and rationalism, Marxism and fascism, laissez-faire capitalism and liberal secularism—there is an opening for the preaching of the gospel of Jesus Christ in a way that has not existed for some time.

It is as if we as a people are spiritually suffocating at some deep level, desperate for some reason to keep going on with our lives, and then we rediscover the church that has always been there. We dare to open its doors and walk back into its expansive sacred space, and suddenly we find that our spirits can breathe again.

This is true for many of the people, I believe, who are sitting in the pews of our churches today. If they have stayed when others have left, it is because they want to be here, they want the church in their lives. They need to have the sacraments and to hear the Good News of Jesus Christ preached to them; they need to receive the church's spiritual support in their personal trials and struggles; and whether they consciously know it or not, they desperately long for the consolation and peace and healing power that are waiting for them in the sacrament of penance.

A Light in the Darkness

A few years ago the Korean Catholic youth groups of the New York metropolitan region sponsored a large retreat for high school students in the Catskill Mountains. Because there were over three hundred young people present, the organizers had arranged to have a number of priests come for an evening reconciliation service. But once private confessions started after the communal part of the service, something unexpected happened. Almost all the teens wanted to go to confession. And as they talked with the priests, many started opening up and going into depth about serious issues that were troubling their souls.

As the night progressed and the numbers of youth waiting for the sacrament did not decrease, some of the priests phoned back to their rectories to say that they were going to be staying over at the retreat until the next day. And a couple of priests actually heard confessions all through the night. They were still there, dressed in their albs and stoles, ministering to the young people when the morning dawned!

I cannot think of a more appropriate image to describe

the vital need for the sacrament of penance in the church's ministry today. The church ventures out into the darkness of our modern world, bearing the *lumen Christi*, the paschal candle, which is the light of Christ. This light shines forth with the brilliance of the Holy Spirit, which is that Easter gift of peace that Christ bestowed on the apostles in the Upper Room and through them on all the followers of Christ. The power of the *lumen Christi* radiates, to be sure, from all the sacraments, preaching and works of the church. But when the night closes in for an individual person, I think it is the sacrament of penance that can best serve as a sort of portable lamp, directly shining the rays of God's healing and grace into the spiritual darkness of the soul.

To fulfill the church's mission of bringing Christ to the modern world—the enormous challenge of the new evangelization—I believe it would help greatly if more priests were found at sunrise, dressed in alb and stole, having heard the confessions of wounded, sinful and struggling Christians throughout the long, dark hours of the night. "You will do well to be attentive to this [prophetic message] as to a lamp shining in a dark place, until the day dawns and the morning star rises in your hearts" (2 Peter 1:19).

CHAPTER TWO

The Sacrament for Contemporary Catholics

L et's do a thought experiment. Imagine for a moment that a young man walks into an RCIA group with absolutely no knowledge of Catholicism. He is a bright, thoughtful fellow who is in touch with the typical needs and desires of his contemporaries. The catechist is describing vividly how the Catholic church has a religious practice that helps people who are in the midst of spiritual, emotional and other crises, enabling them to resolve their guilt, their pain and their despair. At the same time it aids those seeking moral conversion and ongoing spiritual growth.

This practice is personal and private: just the priest and the person involved, one on one. Moreover, it is not a fixed rite in which someone merely watches the minister perform sacred actions and recite some prayers. No, it is profoundly relational and dialogical: The person talks and the priest listens, the priest talks and the person listens, and at times each poses questions to the other or they engage in conversation. And apart from the liturgical formulas at the beginning and the end of the rite, none of this dialogue follows a predetermined script or a set time limit. The person simply bares his or her soul, protected by a seal of confidentiality that is absolutely inviolable, and the priest responds, guided by the

Holy Spirit and the church's teaching. What results is a true personal encounter at the deepest level imaginable: sometimes challenging and direct and at other times peaceful and consoling, leading now to tears and embraces, now to quiet nods of understanding and reassurance.

Warming to her topic, the catechist continues. This religious practice, she says, is extremely flexible and adaptable. It normally takes place in a church, but even then there is no fixed spot for it: The rite can be celebrated in a reconciliation room or in the sacristy, facing the priest in a comfortable chair or kneeling anonymously in a quiet dark confessional, or maybe just sitting alongside a priest in a pew after Mass. And when not performed in the church, it can take place in private homes or out on the street, in airports or automobiles, in convalescent facilities or prison cells, on battlefields or in hospital emergency rooms—and yes, as recounted in the last chapter, even in the back room of a bar!

In fact, a priest can perform this rite with a penitent while casual passersby are completely unaware of it. Yet wherever it is celebrated, its effects can be life-changing, consoling and healing at a depth of a person's soul that medicine, psychotherapy and counseling strive with difficulty to reach.

At this point the young man, who has been intently listening, bursts out: "What is this unique rite that the Catholic church possesses? It sounds to me like the most relevant and needed approach for contemporary men and women! Tell me the name of this wonderfully modern religious practice that must be so appreciated and so popular among Catholics!" The catechist pauses, half smiling, and then replies, "It is called the sacrament of penance."

Three Models

Why does penance have such a "bad rep," to use the jargon of the day? Why on Saturday afternoons are the phones in rectories not ringing off the hooks with Catholics anxious to know the times for confession, just as they are on Sundays with people inquiring about times for Mass? With all the attributes just mentioned—personal and private, relational and dialogical, spontaneous and flexible, healing and consoling—penance should be *the* sacrament for contemporary society. So why do so many Catholics avoid it like the plague? Why do even faithfully practicing Catholics, who would never think of missing Sunday Mass, admit in a slightly apologetic tone, if they are ever asked, that they only get to confession once or twice a year?

To begin to answer these questions, we should recall what the Second Vatican Council and its accompanying liturgical renewal taught about the sacrament of penance. We can sum up its teaching in three notions: Penance is a sacrament of *healing*, of *forgiveness* and of *reconciliation*. As with many areas of Catholic life, Vatican II did not try to prioritize these different aspects of the sacrament; rather, it presented them together in a balanced, unified approach. This means that we can use three different though complementary models for describing the effects of the sacrament of penance.

The *therapeutic* model, as we might call it, refers to the sacrament as a spiritual remedy for healing the wounds of sin and restoring the sinner to the fullness of divine life, called the state of sanctifying grace. In this model the priest functions in the role of doctor or healer of souls. The image from the Gospels that fits this model well is that of Jesus' pity for the suffering and his miracles to relieve their affliction: the paralytic lowered through the roof, the man born blind, the

23

leper cleansed on the road. When Jesus heals, he cures both the body and the soul: "Take up your mat and walk…Your sins are forgiven.…Your faith has saved you" (see Luke 5:17–26 and similar passages).

The *judicial* model speaks of penance as a sacrament in which the sinner is forgiven, the guilt of sin pardoned and the eternal punishment due to grave sin remitted. The penitent enters confession as the defendant "guilty as charged" but walks out a free man or woman. In the judicial model the priest confessor fills the role of judge of souls, exercising the awesome power that Christ conferred on the church in the person of Saint Peter "to loose and to bind" sins: "Whatever you bind on earth will be bound in heaven, and whatever you loose on earth will be loosed in heaven" (Matthew 16:19).

The image from the Gospels best suited to depict this model is of Jesus' calling all to repentance and conversion, claiming divine authority both to forgive sins and to convict of sin in view of the coming kingdom of God. Jesus forgives the woman caught in adultery, the Pharisee Nicodemus, Zacchaeus the tax collector and the woman who washes his feet with her tears and dries them with her hair, because of their true sorrow for their sins and their faith in him as God's anointed. But Jesus convicts the scribes, the lawyers and the Pharisees—indeed, the entire cities of Chorazin, Bethsaida and Capernaum (see Matthew 11:21–24)—for their hypocrisy, their hardness of heart and their refusal to believe in him.

Finally, the *relational* model describes penance as the sacrament that reconciles the alienated sinner both with God, who has been offended by the sin, and with the Christian community, which has been harmed by the sin. Here the priest has the role of reconciler or mediator who restores the sinner to full communion with God in Christ and, by so doing, to full communion with the body of Christ, the church.

This model resonates powerfully with the image of a merciful, caring God portrayed in some of Jesus' most moving parables. He is the shepherd who seeks the lost sheep and carries it home on his shoulders (Luke 15:3–7). He is the Good Samaritan, who rescues the man lying on the side of the road and brings him to the inn to be cared for. The patristic writers saw the inn as a figure for the church; thus the parable conveys the idea of returning to communion with the body of Christ (see Luke 10:29–37). Most of all, God is the forgiving father who rushes out to welcome back his Prodigal Son but also seeks to reconcile the jealous older brother (see Luke 15:11–32).

The introduction to the renewed *Rite of Penance,* which Pope Paul VI promulgated in 1973, summed up well these three complementary models—the therapeutic, the judicial and the relational—with their three different understandings of the role of the priest in confession:

> In order to fulfill his ministry properly and faithfully the confessor should understand the disorders of souls and apply the appropriate remedies to them [therapeutic model]. He should fulfill his office of judge wisely and should acquire the knowledge and prudence necessary for this task by serious study, guided by the teaching authority of the Church and especially by fervent prayer to God [judicial model]....
>
> By receiving the repentant sinner and leading him to the light of the truth the confessor fulfills a paternal function: he reveals the heart of the Father and shows the image of Christ the Good Shepherd. He should keep in mind that he has been entrusted with the ministry of Christ, who mercifully accomplished the saving work of man's redemption

and who is present by his power in the sacraments [relational model].[1]

So why the bad reputation for the sacrament of penance? Perhaps it is because too many Catholics are locked into a view of the sacrament that puts all the emphasis on the judicial model and none on the therapeutic and relational models. Though forty years of sacramental catechesis since Vatican II have taken pains to emphasize the role of the priest as healer and reconciler, many people still seem to see him simply as a judge. And even then, their focus appears to be on the element of judgment rather than on the liberating experience of forgiveness. They claim an aversion to confessing their sins to a priest. But they never mention the tremendous consolation that can follow when the priest says to them at the end those awesome words, bearing an assurance of forgiveness that comes from Christ himself: "And I absolve you from your sins in the name of the Father and of the Son and of the Holy Spirit."

I discussed this conundrum recently with a sister who is director of religious education in an educated suburban parish. "I know the excellent training you are giving your students in preparation for the sacrament of penance, stressing all the themes of healing, forgiveness and reconciliation that were promoted by the Council. Why in so many of our parishes hasn't it 'taken'?" I asked. "Why do some kids make their first penance at age seven and then come back for their 'second penance' when they are about to be confirmed?"

Sister Ann thought pensively for a moment and then replied: "The problem is that there are so many forces working against us." She explained that even though catechists and priests may work hard to make the first confession a kind, inviting and personal experience, many parents never bring their children back to receive the sacrament again. The first positive celebration of the sacrament of healing, forgiveness and reconciliation never has a chance to mature into a lifelong habit of frequenting penance.

Some parents may even use confession as a punishment. When a child does something seriously wrong, the mother or father brings him or her down to the church and orders, "Now go in and tell the priest you're sorry for what you did!"

But the most powerful negative message that many parents send their children about penance, said Sister Ann, is the self-evident fact that they rarely, if ever, make use of the sacrament themselves. She concluded, "They're sending a subliminal message to their kids all the time: This is not something in our religion that matters."

Does the reluctance of so many Catholics to make regular use of the sacrament of penance point to a deeper spiritual problem that pervades our society as well as our church? Do we modern-day Catholics believe that we need a sacrament of forgiveness? Do we actually feel guilty for doing something sinfully wrong?

Most priests can chuckle about the penitent who comes into the confessional really wanting to confess someone else's sins, such as the husband or wife who goes on and on about all the failings and insensitivities of his or her spouse until the priest gently asks, "But what are your sins that you want to confess?" Do such humorous anecdotes point to a more serious phenomenon: Have contemporary Catholics concluded that ultimately they are not to blame for their actions?

Clearly, penance is a sacrament that demands an authentic grasp of human freedom and responsibility. Only a person who is free can commit a morally culpable action. Only one

27

who accepts personal responsibility can confess guilt and seek forgiveness.

As Catholic moral theology has consistently taught, a person cannot be guilty of a sin unless he or she knowingly and freely does something that is objectively evil. In a society of perpetual adolescence, where adults excuse their actions by passing blame onto their family of origin, their present or former spouses, the pressures of business, the negligence of others or just their own base instincts and desires (the "God made me this way" argument), perhaps the question needs to be posed: Are contemporary men and women capable of receiving a sacrament that demands so much personal freedom and responsibility? In a world where everyone believes he or she is a victim, is anyone willing to acknowledge being a deliberate moral actor?

Monsignor Robert McCormick, who ministered to generations of future army officers as a Catholic chaplain at the U.S. Military Academy at West Point from 1947 to 1975, recounts a discussion he once had with some cadets. A Protestant young man commented in a non-malicious way, "Well, you Catholics don't really believe in personal freedom."

Monsignor McCormick shot back: "Just the opposite. Look at the Catholic rite of confession!"

As he recalls, that opening salvo grabbed the group's attention at once. He proceeded to explain: "When Catholics confess their sins in the sacrament of penance, they are acknowledging that they consciously and willingly used their personal freedom in a way that was contrary to God's will and their own authentic good. And when they then state their firm purpose of amendment, they are solemnly resolving to use their personal freedom in the future in a way that will be in accord with God's will and their own authentic good."

Concluded Monsignor McCormick, "The priest cannot make penitents acknowledge their guilt or force them to resolve not to sin again. That can only be done by an individual human being acting out of a deep sense of personal freedom and out of a conviction of personal responsibility for the use of that freedom."

Whatever the cause of the present malaise affecting the sacrament of penance, the thesis of this book is that there is a pressing pastoral challenge to reintroduce the practice of going to confession as a central component in Catholic life and devotion: one of the seven official means that the Lord gave to us as privileged, divinely warranted instruments of his saving grace. This generation of Catholics needs to rediscover penance as a sacrament perfectly suited to modern needs, in all the ways we have mentioned: a religious practice that is personal and private, relational and dialogical, spontaneous and flexible, healing and consoling.

To accomplish that goal, the church needs to find a way to lead Catholics once again to experience the sacrament of penance. Once they personally encounter the Lord's healing, forgiving and reconciling grace, experienced in the unique way that sacramental confession and absolution can mediate it, I truly believe that they will find themselves drawn to this special sacrament as fervently as generations of Catholics before them were.

The Spiritual Versatility of Penance

What are the distinctive aspects of the rite of penance that need to be explained clearly and convincingly in order to achieve this reintroduction of Catholics to the sacrament? One key aspect of penance that is not appreciated enough is its spiritual versatility. The moral scope that this sacrament encompasses is huge.

First both in historical development and in priority, of course, is penance's ability to reconcile baptized Christians to God and the church after grave sin. Indeed, as the *Catechism* reminds us, "Individual and integral confession of grave sins followed by absolution remains the only ordinary means of reconciliation with God and with the Church,"[2] which repeats exactly the citation in canon 960 of the 1983 *Code of Canon Law*.[3]

Some of the most moving confessions that priests hear are by Catholics who have been carrying for years the weight of a mortal sin: the husband who engaged in an adulterous affair that destroyed his marriage, the mother who cannot forgive herself for the abortion she agreed to when she was a young single woman, the man who left the practice of the faith in his youth and now looks back over a wasted life of self-indulgence and spiritual emptiness. Appropriately called in the early church "the second plank [of salvation] after the shipwreck which is the loss of grace"[4] through mortal sin, penance in such cases has a power to forgive and heal and literally bring back to life, both spiritually and emotionally, that is hard to appreciate if one has not been in the shoes of those penitents or of the priests who absolved them.

Interestingly, in my experience such persons often want to confess their sins face-to-face with the priest. It is as if they need to look him in the eye as the tears run down their face and, after the absolution and blessing, to feel his arms around them—the arms of Christ—as he welcomes them back into full communion. In fact, once a young father who chose the anonymity of the screen to confess a very serious sin spontaneously said to me at the end of our long conversation,

"Father, do you mind if I come around and shake your hand?" He came around the portable screen, we embraced, and he wiped tears away as he walked out of the reconciliation room.

Second, and just as important in pastoral practice, is the use of the sacrament of penance to absolve venial sins: those common faults that, according to the Scriptures, the just man commits seven times daily (see Proverbs 24:16; Luke 17:4). Catholics who come to confession every few weeks are not misguided souls obsessed with guilt and fear. Granted, there may have been at times an element of scrupulosity in the popular confessional devotion of preconciliar Catholics, as if they doubted they could avoid falling into mortal sin from one Sunday Mass to the next. But the deeper, authentically Catholic instinct behind the discipline of frequent confession is that the sacrament is a powerful means to overcome habitual moral failings and to grow in the life of grace.

It is true that justification occurs but once, when a sinner receives the free gift of God's grace through faith and baptism. This is the experience of being "born anew" (1 Peter 1:23) in Christ, something which can certainly come through a dramatic adult conversion (the "born again" experience evangelicals like to stress) but which is realized just as surely by receiving sacramental baptism as a child and then persevering in that commitment as one matures (the more common Catholic experience). After justification, however, there comes the lifelong process of drawing closer to God and increasing in grace, which is the task of sanctification. And sanctification is what penance, like all the sacraments, brings about.

For one needing to overcome habitual moral failings and to grow in holiness—and who of us does not fall into that category?—regular confession is as vital as a substance abusers' support group is for a recovering addict. Just as the latter would not dare "go it alone" for an extended period or try to "pick himself up" after a relapse, so a Catholic who is serious about overcoming habits of sin and developing habits of virtue values tremendously the support of the sacramental graces of penance, the assurance of being absolved from one's sins no matter how often one falls and the counsel of a wise priest about how to avoid sinful habits in the future.

The Problem of Evil

Yet still we have not exhausted the spiritual versatility of the sacrament of penance. Its third use is to receive and bury, like a deep spiritual well, the burden of objective sin: all the pains and doubts and fears with which one must struggle in this life. As unlikely a source as the atheistic nineteenth-century German philosopher Friedrich Nietzsche recognized this profoundly significant quality of confession as practiced in the Catholic church. He observed: "After [Martin] Luther had given a wife to the priest, he had to take from him auricular confession; that was psychologically right: but thereby he practically did away with the Christian priest himself, whose profoundest utility has ever consisted in his being a sacred ear, a silent well, a grave for secrets."[5]

Resonating with the Lord's own ministry to suffering people in the Gospels, penance is a formidable tool for "casting out the demons" from our lives: that is, the burden of objective sin that afflicts all of us who are still on the way to our heavenly homeland. What is the difference between "objective" sin and "subjective" sin—or more precisely, between objective, moral and physical evil contrasted with subjective, personal guilt? To my mind, the practical ignorance of many Catholics regarding this primary moral distinction risks trivializing the church's entire understanding of sin, repentance and redemption. Because the point is so important, we must make a slight digression to explain the distinction here.

Objective sin refers to the massive reality of evil in our world in all its manifold aspects: hatred, suffering, guilt, alienation, death. Saint Paul summed up the whole tragic history of our race in one pithy line: "Sin came into the world through one man, and death came through sin, and so death spread to all because all have sinned" (Romans 5:12).

How can so much human pain and suffering be explained by that one primal act of disobedience, that first "original sin"? Theology tries to begin formulating an answer to this question by the notion of subjective sin, which refers to the personal guilt of human beings who, individually and collectively, have perpetuated Adam's disobedience by freely choosing to do wrong. We are born with the guilt of original sin, which we inherit from Adam, but then we make it our own by freely indulging in our own personal sins.

Yet somehow this moral calculus of objective evil and subjective guilt never quite adds up. The Catholic tradition calls it the *mysterium iniquitatis*, or "mystery of evil." Basically "good people," belonging to certain classes or races or nations, give in to venal self-interest and succumb to ethnic and ideological rivalries. The results are monstrous sins of slavery and oppression, murder and genocide, war and persecution and terrorism.

On a smaller scale, the son of an abusive father grows up to become an abuser of his own wife and children; a girl growing up in a home where the mother has different boyfriends sleeping over all the time becomes sexually promiscuous as soon as she enters high school; a corporate executive works seventy hours a week so his family can live in a safe and comfortable town and then watches his marriage and children suffer for lack of a father's presence. Where does the guilt lie in all this human suffering?

An individual suffers personal pain and harm from an explosive temperament or an alcoholic addiction or same-sex attraction. Certainly the person deserves sympathy and support for the heavy burden of an affective disorder attributable perhaps to physiological and environmental causes. But encouraging someone to disclaim any personal responsibility for how he or she responds to this disordered condition (an objective evil) takes away that person's individual freedom and reduces him or her to the status of a victim.

The point is that, in varying degrees that only God can measure, we all approach the sacrament of penance both suffering the effects of objective evil and also subjectively responsible for causing them, victims of "sin and death" as well as its perpetrators, harmed by the offenses of others but never purely innocent bystanders. So I feel strongly that the first priority when approaching the sacrament of penance is simply to honestly surface all the instances of objective sin that one is confronting in one's life.

"What are the obstacles keeping you from getting closer to God and experiencing his grace and peace more powerfully in your life?" is how I often put the question to penitents who tell me they do not know what to confess. The matter of sorting out the individual's subjective guilt can follow. But just as a patient does not start out by explaining to the doctor why his back pains or his ulcers are not his fault but rather implores the doctor to relieve his pain, so I believe a penitent should approach Christ and his church first of all with the attitude of humbly begging God's healing of all the effects of evil in one's life. "Jesus, son of David, have mercy on me!" This sincere, plaintive cry, uttered by the blind beggar Bartimaeus (see Mark 10:47), sums up in my mind the attitude of the Christian approaching the font of divine mercy in confession.

When Catholics use the sacrament of penance in this way, the results can be powerful and liberating. "I don't know who's to blame, but my wife and I are becoming more and more distant, and I don't know what to do." "My husband passed away recently, and I am torn by guilt. On the one hand I miss him terribly, but on the other hand I am relieved to be free from his verbal abuse and anger." "I try to come to Mass and pray, but God just does not seem to answer, so I have given up on going to church."

Starting from such honest, soul-searching confessions as these, I have seen real reconciliation and peace follow in the lives of penitents. The question of subjective guilt has to be dealt with, of course. But it does not always have to be the starting point, or even the dominant motivation, for approaching Christ, the divine healer of bodies and souls, in the sacrament of penance.

The account of Jesus' meeting with the woman caught in adultery illustrates this progression from objective evil to subjective sin in a beautiful way and shows how Christ comes to save the sinner from both. First Jesus saves the frightened woman from the objective evil of impending vengeance and death, represented by the crowd ready to stone her: "Let anyone among you who is without sin be the first to throw a stone at her." Then he shows the woman the merciful face of God, who comes not to condemn her but to forgive her and restore her to life: "Woman, where are they? Has no one condemned you?…Neither do I condemn you." And only at the end does he address the question of her personal guilt: "Go your way, and from now on do not sin again" (see John 8:1–11).

The Role of the Priest-Confessor

Another distinctive aspect of penance that needs to be clarified for Catholics seeking to be re-introduced to this sacrament is the unique role the priest plays. In chapter four we will take up the most challenging objection in this regard: namely, why does one have to confess one's sins to a priest at all? But here we deal simply with the need for Catholics to be reeducated about the traditional practice of "choosing a confessor."

It is interesting that the pre-conciliar church—not especially noted for extolling the virtue of private options in the religious realm—nevertheless took pains to defend the right of penitents to choose the priest to whom they would bare their consciences. In practical terms, this meant that two or more priests from a parish would usually hear confessions on a Saturday afternoon, sometimes assisted by visiting priests. Even if a penitent's criterion for selection was simply which priest had the shorter line, the possibility of choice was preserved.

Religious communities and cloistered convents observed this principle by making provision for "extern confessors" to come in from time to time. Thus the monks or brothers or nuns would not be compelled to confess to the resident chaplain or a priest from their own religious community.

The wisdom of the church's custom is clear. In a religious practice that is so personal, confidential and relational, it is a tremendous help to be able to freely choose the priest in whose hands you will place the spiritual welfare of your soul. How should a Catholic decide what priest to go to in confession?

The choice can be made for purely subjective reasons: you feel you can talk to this priest, he strikes you as compassionate and insightful, or he has personal experience or expertise in dealing with your primary moral challenge. (For example, recovering alcoholics may feel a special bond with a priest who is a fellow member of Alcoholics Anonymous.) A confessor may even be chosen for reasons that appear rather arbitrary: He is the pastor or the assistant, he is a diocesan priest or a religious priest, he is old or young, you share the same ethnic background or come from the same part of the country, and so on. (Looking at confessors I have chosen over the course of my priesthood, I realize I am partial to priests over eighty!)

However, there are three objective criteria that should be followed in selecting the regular confessor with whom one will share one's deepest struggles and to whom one will turn for moral guidance. These are holiness, wisdom and fidelity.

First of all, the priest-confessor must be holy. That does not mean he has to be a saint (though it helps—Saint Teresa of Avila picked Saint John of the Cross). But he must be a man of God who is sincerely striving for holiness and who has gained at least some degree of self-mastery in the moral life. Just as you would not feel comfortable taking golf lessons from a hacker with a 30 handicap or registering for a weight-loss program with a trainer who is a hundred pounds overweight, it could be risky seeking regular moral instruction from a person who is floundering in serious sin himself or, even worse, who has no desire to pursue a righteous way of life.

Secondly, the priest confessor should be wise. There is an attractive innocence about certain Christians. They possess a childlike faith and a non-reflective, almost naïve instinct for doing good. A priest in confession, however, needs to be a discerning spiritual judge and a wise doctor of souls. While it is certainly not required that he be a moral theologian, he must possess a sound knowledge of the church's teaching and prudent insight into human behavior. As the Gospels relate, Jesus was a teacher who knew what was in men's hearts (see Luke 9:47; John 2:24–25), and the priest in confession is called to imitate to the best of his ability this attentiveness and insight into the complexities of the human soul.

The third objective criterion is one that cannot be ignored. The priest-confessor must be a man of fidelity, obedient to the law of God and the church's teaching. As the *Catechism* says, "the confessor is not the master of God's forgiveness, but its servant."[6] He must truly desire to be, as explicitly as did the great third-century theologian Origen, a *vir ecclesiasticus*: that is, a "man of the Church."

It would seem self-evident that when one approaches a Catholic priest in confession, one will find someone who "love[s] the truth" and is "faithful to the Magisterium of the Church,"[7] according to the moral norms contained in Scripture and Tradition. Unfortunately, just as some lay people disastrously misinterpreted Vatican II's teaching on the rights of individual conscience, taking it to mean virtual emancipation from the demands of God's revelation and the church's authoritative teaching, some priests did the same. I still vividly recall seeking guidance in confession back in the 1970s about a serious moral issue I was confronting. After advising me to pursue a course that I knew was not in accord with Catholic moral teaching, this priest said in closing that he would prefer that I "not quote him"—a clear tip-off to me that this was not a confessor I could trust.

The late Cardinal James Hickey once said to a group of seminarians at Theological College, the major seminary attached to Catholic University in Washington, D.C.: "The people of God have a right to hear the teaching of the church." That applies in the pulpit, in Catholic schools and universities and certainly in that most sacred internal forum of the confessional.

Flexibility and Accessibility

A final distinctive aspect of penance is its practical flexibility and accessibility. I believe that in an age that so values convenience and easy access—with cell phones, twenty-four-hour banking and online technical support—Catholics need to rediscover just how accessible and flexible is the rite of penance.

The normal location for celebrating this rite is in the church, whether in a communal liturgical service or privately in the reconciliation room or confessional, since this is one of the church's official acts by which it sanctifies the Christian people. But whereas couples need the permission of the local bishop to celebrate marriage outside of the church and baptism is performed outside of the church only in cases of necessity or emergency, a priest has wide latitude in deciding an appropriate spot for administering the sacrament of penance. I have heard confessions for parishioners in the sacristy before or after Mass, in the rectory or on a walk around the parish grounds. I have given absolution in airports and in cars, while visiting patients in hospitals or bringing Communion to the sick and elderly in their homes.

My favorite example of a spontaneous confession happened on a visit to Franciscan University in Steubenville, Ohio. I was hurriedly walking, huffing and puffing, up the notoriously steep hill leading to the main campus, with my alb for Mass over my shoulder, when a car pulled over as it passed by me. Thinking a considerate student had taken pity on me and was about to offer me a ride, I hastened up to the car. A young man rolled down the window and said, "Father, got time for a quick confession?" I got in the front seat and replied, "Yes, but you have to promise then to drive me up to the chapel so I won't be late for Mass!"

Basilicas, shrines and other pilgrimage sites are especially good places to celebrate the sacrament of penance for a couple of reasons. First of all, these churches often enlist the services of a number of wise, experienced priests who make it their special ministry to counsel the many visitors who come to pray. Secondly, they make the sacrament of penance easily available, usually offering confessions for one or two periods daily and in some places providing confessors fluent in several languages. For example, confessions are heard in over ten modern languages in St. Peter's Basilica in Rome and in the reconciliation chapel at Lourdes, France.

Knowing that one can easily receive the sacrament of penance during the week in, for example, Washington (National Shrine of the Immaculate Conception), Los Angeles (Cathedral of Our Lady of the Angels) or New York (St. Patrick's Cathedral), many local residents and workers as well as out-of-town visitors will slip into these urban cathedrals and basilicas to go to confession. I recall walking into the reconciliation chapel in the crypt church of the National Shrine in Washington and being edified to see a bishop, in clerical suit and pectoral cross, sitting in line for his turn to see the priest.

Special Occasions for Penance

In addition to its accessibility in many different kinds of places, penance can also be flexibly adapted to many different occasions and times in people's lives. For teenagers on an Emmaus or Search retreat, or for adults making a Cursillo or Marriage Encounter weekend or perhaps a retreat sponsored by Rachel's Vineyard (for post-abortion healing) or Theos (for bereavement support), confession often becomes the dramatic high point. The candidate pours out his or her soul to a priest especially prepared to minister at this critical spiritual moment.

A wise pastor of souls makes confession available immediately after every wedding rehearsal. This gives the bride and groom a chance to begin their married vocation free of sin and ready to be filled with the graces that Christian marriage offers them, just as it gives their bridal party and families an opportunity to make a good confession and receive Communion worthily.

High school and college chaplains, in particular, know that they have access to young people at times when they are facing some of the biggest moral challenges of their lives. Whether it is confessions offered to Catholic high school students in a gym during Advent or Lent or the sacrament celebrated privately in a Newman Center or campus ministry lounge, the right words of counsel to a young person trying to set his or her moral rudder in a frighteningly secular and pagan environment can literally save a life, both spiritually and physically. In a similar way priests who visit the sick in hospitals, the dying in hospices or inmates in prisons bring healing and forgiveness to people at a time when the consolation this can afford is magnified a hundredfold.

But perhaps the most dramatic witness to the way in which penance can be immediately accessible to people in need—the church's version of a "first responder" sacrament, if you will—are the stories of priests who have ministered to people in the midst of catastrophic crises. Father Kevin Smith was sitting in his rectory at St. Rose of Lima Church in Massapequa, Long Island, New York, on September 11, 2001. A chaplain with the Nassau County Fire Department, he rushed into New York with his brother, a New York City fire-fighter, as both their pagers called them to duty after the terrorist attack on the World Trade Center. He was the priest who found and blessed the body of Father Mychal Judge, the New York City fire chaplain who died from debris falling from the Twin Towers, and he enlisted a group of firefighters to carry Father Judge's body over to St. Peter's Catholic Church. A photographer captured the moving scene of debris-covered firefighters carrying in their arms a white-haired priest, still wearing his firefighter's uniform. This is how Father Smith describes what he did for the rest of that awful day and into the night:

> I stayed close to the main command center to see if I was needed. From time to time they would find another uniformed person in the collapse and ask me to come to bless the body and say a prayer before the body was removed to the temporary morgue. All during this time I was talking to the rescuers, some of them survivors of both collapses. They were wondering why they were spared and the person right behind them was lost.… I heard a lot of confessions that day and many of them including the ironworkers were asking for a blessing when they saw me. Throughout the night I worked on the pile shoulder to shoulder with police, fire, and medical rescue.… The one thing I heard so many times from the rescuers that night

was, "Hey Father, thanks for being down here with us, it really means a lot."[8]

The line he writes after this is to me powerfully moving. Father Smith reflects on that hellish day at Ground Zero and says simply, almost abruptly, "It felt great to be a priest." In the midst of the greatest evil, in a place of death stemming from an unimaginable abyss of sin and hatred, the church's minister comes offering the only response that truly makes a difference: the compassionate heart of Christ, a priest's blessing and the words of absolution in the sacrament of penance.

CHAPTER THREE

Popular Reasons for Avoiding Confession (and Why They Are Wrong)

I have heard many reasons and rationalizations for not confessing one's sins to a priest and seeking absolution. It seems that they all ultimately reduce to three categories. One set of objections is voiced by those who feel embarrassment and shame about acknowledging their private moral failures and who fear how the priest will respond. Another line of reasoning is employed by those who just seem uncertain about the practice of going to confession nowadays, whether because they feel uncomfortable with the revised approach to receiving the sacrament or they are not clear anymore about what exactly qualify as sins "worth confessing." A third type of argument comes from those who say that they are "basically good persons" who don't really need to receive the sacrament of penance. Let's consider each of these sets of objections.

Shame and Fear

No matter how personable and inviting the rite of penance may become, it seems unavoidable that at least on some occasions people are going to experience embarrassment and guilt when they have to admit aloud to another person their sinful acts. When hearing high school confessions, for example, it is not unusual to listen to a recitation that goes something like,

"I fought with my sister, I disobeyed my parents, I gossiped, I had sex with my boyfriend, I missed my daily prayers...." The hope seems to be that by sandwiching a grave sin amidst offenses that seem less significant, the priest might be induced to overlook the really bad one!

Sometimes one encounters with older penitents a confessional formula that must have been taught in some former catechetical programs (though I am not familiar with them). The person will say: "Bless me, Father, for I have sinned. I accuse myself of violating the second, third, sixth and eighth commandments." In such a case I reply, "How frequently do you fail to observe the second, third and eighth commandments? And could you give me a few more specifics about the way you violated the sixth?!"

In a fundamental sense, of course, there is something right and salutary about the feelings of embarrassment and guilt couched in these confessions. They mirror the response of Adam and Eve after their fall, when they hid in the bushes at the sound of God's voice, ashamed at their now-recognized nakedness (see Genesis 3:8–10). Shame is the proper reaction to an awareness of personal sin; it is a sign of a moral conscience that is alive.

Though "Catholic guilt" has been much maligned over the last forty years, an appropriate and balanced sense of guilt for the wrong that we have done is as necessary for spiritual maturity as a sense of responsibility for one's actions is for personal maturity. The problem arises when our sense of embarrassment and shame impedes us from making a full and honest confession. If we don't expose the infected wound to the surgeon's skilled hand, he is unable to treat it. For the same reason, the church has traditionally taught that Catholics are bound to make—to cite the terminology of the

Council of Trent—a complete or "integral" confession of all serious sins (*integram peccatorum confessionem*), confessing them "specifically and individually" (*in specie ac singillatim*) to a priest in the sacrament of penance.[1]

The point is not to make the penitent wallow in guilt or to take a prurient interest in the specifics of another's moral failings. Rather, the aim is to apply the healing balm of sacramental grace on precisely that part of our moral physiognomy that has suffered the wound of sin. Interestingly, both the Council of Trent meeting in 1551 and the *Catechism of the Catholic Church*, published in 1992, cite a line from Saint Jerome of the fourth century that uses precisely this medical analogy to explain the necessity of confessing one's sins to a priest. Says Saint Jerome, "For if the sick person is too ashamed to show his wound to the doctor, the medicine cannot heal what it does not know."[2]

Open to Healing

I heard a charming story once from an elderly Sister of Saint Ann living in Victoria, British Columbia, that illustrates this point well. Sister Mary Ida Brasseur served in education and pastoral work in the Alaska mission from 1946 to 1988. For a while she and another sister were involved in full-time rural ministry from their base in Anchorage. Each weekend they would fly to some far-flung outpost where they would catechize and minister to the people gathered for Sunday Mass.

One weekend the destination was Dillingham on Alaska's west coast. It was summer, when the salmon were running in the Yukon River, so the Inuits would leave their fishing camps and travel by boat down to Dillingham to go to church. That Sunday, however, the priest did not arrive.

Sister Ida recalls how disappointed an older Inuit woman was. She had come down from the camp specifically to go to confession and then attend Mass. She confided to the French Canadian nun how difficult it had always been for her to confess her sins to the priest in the sacrament of penance.

Sister Ida replied, "When you go to the doctor, you don't like having to take off your coat and all your clothes, right?"

The Inuit woman nodded.

"But you know that if you don't do that, the doctor isn't going to be able to help you get better. It is the very same way with the priest in confession."

Consoled by this explanation, the old woman then began sharing her moral concerns and personal failings with the nun. When she was finished, Sister Ida replied, "God hears you. Tell him you are truly sorry. And the next time the priest comes, say to him in confession what you just told me and receive absolution." Then she added, "But for now, come and join us in the prayer service that we will lead for all who have gathered here."

The Inuit woman went away with a newfound sense of peace about how to confess her sins to the priest in the sacrament of confession.

Father Kevin Royal, rector of St. John Fisher Seminary Residence in Stamford, Connecticut, describes this essential attitude of honesty and openness in the sacrament of penance as the virtue of "transparency." His constant refrain to the seminarians is "We must be absolutely transparent. Secrecy with our confessor and spiritual director is deadly, while transparency is the path of humility and invitation to grace. It is no accident that God's first act of creation is 'Let there be light.' Shining light on our sin and darkness is re-creation."

His exhortation is right on target. We must hide nothing. We should be transparent to the Lord, who is present in the person of the priest, when we bring our sins to the church's solemn and private forum of sacramental confession. If we are discreet or equivocating in describing our moral failings, we certainly do not keep them hidden from God—for he alone "tests the mind and searches the heart" (see Jeremiah 17:10)—but we make it more difficult for the church's minister to shine the light of grace into the dark recesses of our souls so that we may live once more illuminated by Christ's truth.

I can honestly say that there are no spiritual crises or moral struggles or major dilemmas that I have faced that I did not share with a priest in confession. And I am convinced that on more than one occasion that has saved my life—spiritually, emotionally and physically.

What Will Father Say?

There is a related objection that is more easily dealt with. Some Catholics will say that they avoid the sacrament of penance because they fear the priest's response. For example, one older woman recounts that she once told her parish priest in confession that she was at times missing Sunday Mass. She explained that she was a new mother nursing a sickly infant, and her husband was frequently away on business. The priest's gruff response—that she should "try harder"—rankles in her memory fifty years later!

Whatever the shortcomings of a previous generation of priests in their role as healers and reconcilers in confession, I honestly believe that pastoral insensitivity in the sacrament of penance is not a charge we can fairly level against the majority of confessors today. When in 1984 Pope John Paul II issued his apostolic exhortation on reconciliation and penance, *Reconciliatio et Paenitentia*, he invoked in the very first chapter the image of the forgiving father in the parable of the Prodigal Son as the model for the church's reconciling ministry: "The most striking element of the parable is the father's festive and loving welcome of the returning son: it is a sign of the mercy of God who is always willing to forgive.… The parable of the Prodigal Son is above all the story of the inexpressible love of a Father—God—who offers to his son when he comes back to him the gift of full reconciliation."[3]

Today's priests have heeded the advice of the Pope John Paul II well, I believe, in adopting the compassionate and forgiving father as the primary model for how to receive sinners who approach the church for reconciliation. If priests make errors in judgment in the confessional, in fact, I suspect they more often err in the direction of being too tolerant in responding to sins rather than being overly severe.

This is not to say, however, that confessors will always utter the most appropriate or helpful words of counsel. Sometimes they are rushed, or inattentive or just not that insightful on the specific moral point one is raising. But there is one practical thing that a penitent can do to help the priest respond beneficially: give him some feedback, and don't hesitate to ask questions! If the priest's words in reply to your confession reveal that he has not understood fully the circumstances of a sin you mentioned or the nature of a moral problem you raised, then tell him this candidly and provide the necessary clarification so that he can make a more informed judgment.

The example just mentioned of missing Sunday Mass is a good example. The obligation to attend Mass on the Lord's Day is without doubt a grave matter. When a student in class

or a parishioner in a discussion asks me, sometimes face-
tiously, whether or not he or she will "go to hell" for missing
Sunday Mass, I do not hesitate to respond in total earnest:

> I sincerely believe that if without any good reason I chose
> to just "blow off" going to Mass one Sunday, yes, I would
> be endangering the salvation of my eternal soul. Because
> having been given the grace to believe that the Mass is the
> re-presentation of the sacrifice by which Christ the
> redeemer has saved my soul, my refusal to join the church
> in its weekly commemoration of Christ's death and resur-
> rection through the breaking of the bread, as Christians
> have done every Sunday since the time of the apostles,
> would indicate clearly that *in my case* I was rejecting my
> faith in Christ.

But that is not what I say in the confessional to the senior cit-
izen who explains that she missed Mass because she did not
feel right leaving a sick husband; or to the middle school student who doesn't come to church because his parents don't
bring him; or to the marginal Catholic who clearly has no idea
why Sunday Mass is so important.

In the first case there is a moral impossibility for the wife
to come to church, because it would be wrong for her to neg-
lect her husband in need; in the second case there is a physical impossibility on the part of the child, since presumably he
does not have another way to get to church; and in the final
case there appears to be lacking the full knowledge needed to
commit a mortal sin.

My point is that a priest is grateful when a penitent helps
him understand the full context of the sins committed, so that
the priest can make an appropriate judgment and give specific, proper advice. For unlike the doctor who can draw upon
x-rays and blood tests in planning a patient's course of

treatment, the confessor must make his moral diagnosis relying entirely upon how the penitent describes the state of his own soul.

The Uncomfortable and Uncertain

A second set of reasons is voiced by those who have no objection in principle to confessing their sins to the priest but who are either uncomfortable with the more flexible form of the rite of penance since Vatican II or are uncertain about what qualifies these days as sins "worth confessing." This group may include Catholics who attend Mass faithfully every Sunday and indeed some who in an earlier time would have gone to confession weekly. Now they acknowledge with almost a guilty air that they "might receive the sacrament of penance once or twice a year."

The first response here is simply to point out, "If you're uncomfortable with some of the new forms that the rite of penance can take, then stick with the old one!" There is nothing wrong with slipping into the confessional and beginning with the tried and true formula: "Bless me, Father, for I have sinned. It has been three months since my last confession. These are my sins.…"

Displaying a pastoral wisdom and understanding that was not always present in the introduction of other liturgical changes after Vatican II, the church made available a number of new options in the rite of penance, but it did not suppress the form of the rite that had existed for years. Thus, penitents could now confess their sins by speaking to the priest informally and face-to-face. They could use various new formulas for the Act of Contrition or compose a prayer of sorrow for sin in their own words. They could receive the sacrament, if they wished, as part of a communal penance liturgy that would include hymns, prayers, Scripture readings and a homily. And even when the sacrament was administered privately, the priest was encouraged to include some of these elements, such as a brief reading from Scripture, a psalm response or at least some spontaneous prayer. But by the same token, if a Catholic preferred "the old way," he or she was entitled to confess sins anonymously to the priest behind the screen, using the set formulas and the traditional Act of Contrition memorized as a child. And that remains the case today.

The other difficulty frequently raised by this group of Catholics is the uncertainty they feel about exactly what kind of sins are supposed to be confessed to a priest these days. This is the more interesting objection, reflecting an underlying attitude toward the sacrament of penance that to my mind has remained remarkably constant since before Vatican II. What I am referring to is a *minimalist* approach toward Christian morality, which inevitably carries over into one's examination of conscience prior to confession.

The prevalent attitude seems to be "What are the rules that have to be observed in order to be a good Christian and a faithful Catholic?" When one breaks these rules, one acknowledges the infractions to the priest in the sacrament of penance and receives absolution. The interesting thing about the minimalist approach is that it can be found both among the morally scrupulous and the morally lax!

Dissent and Confusion

Up to the Second Vatican Council, most people saw a Catholic church that demanded adherence to a fairly rigorous code of moral behavior; both confessing members and outsiders alike recognized this. Much anecdotal evidence can be presented to support this assertion, but a story I like to cite concerns a bright Southern Baptist undergraduate at Georgetown University in the sixties. His essays caught the attention of his young Jesuit philosophy professor. The teacher took his promising student out to a nearby restaurant and asked him if he had ever considered studying for the priesthood.

The student, who recalls being flattered by the offer, had to reply to the surprised Jesuit, "Don't you think I have to become a Catholic first?" And he remembers adding, "I don't know; the rules [in the Catholic church] are pretty tight!"

This Georgetown undergrad went on to become the only U.S. president to receive a degree from a Catholic university—Bill Clinton. This poses a fascinating piece of presidential trivia. Assuming that no one ever proposed a clerical career to John Kennedy, Bill Clinton may be the only president in the nation's history to have been encouraged to consider a vocation to the priesthood![4]

As is well known, this rigorous approach to morality among Catholics changed rapidly in the sixties and seventies. Some rules governing Catholic behavior were formally mitigated by church authority: for example, the obligation "under pain of sin" to abstain from meat on all Fridays. Many moral norms became confused in the popular consciousness of Catholics, in part because of misleading advice by pastors; a deficient catechesis; and widely publicized dissent by leading theologians, priests and religious.

The result was that the rigorist, often scrupulous Catholic conscience of the forties, fifties and early sixties gave way to the lenient, often lax conscience of Catholics in the late sixties, seventies and eighties. Suddenly, missing Sunday Mass was not a big deal, younger Catholics embraced the contraceptive lifestyle of the modern American family as widely as their parents' generation had faithfully resisted it and priests were telling divorced and civilly remarried Catholics privately that they were morally inculpable if they believed in their conscience that their first marriage was invalid. (Incidentally, this latter position is a gross misinterpretation of what is referred to as the "internal forum solution," which properly refers to the permission in certain circumstances for Catholics in an irregular marriage to receive the sacraments if they are willing to live "as brother and sister.")

The fascinating point, however, is that the underlying attitude governing popular thinking about morality, both before and after Vatican II, was and still is minimalist! Pre–Vatican II Catholics saw many things as seriously sinful and held themselves to an exacting standard of moral behavior. So they were inclined to use the sacrament of penance regularly to confess their offenses and were quick to abstain from receiving Holy Communion. Post–Vatican II Catholics, on the other hand, have taken a more tolerant view of what constitutes grave sin and have been quick to excuse themselves from moral precepts because of mitigating personal circumstances. They receive the sacrament of penance infrequently, if at all, but always come up to receive the Eucharist at Mass. And when they confess their sins, they normally mention personal failings in their relationships with others—for example, getting angry, being jealous or critical, gossiping and lying— yet might omit sins such as seldom attending Sunday Mass or cohabiting with a boyfriend or girlfriend.

Both cases reflect a minimalist approach: "When I break some rule, then I confess it to a priest." The difference is that the former, rigorist Catholic believed in a lot more rules that were easily broken, whereas the present, lax Catholic subscribes to fewer rules, and these seem much more difficult to break in a morally significant way.

This explains, I believe, why some Catholics today will say in good faith that they really don't know what they are supposed to confess. They wonder whether a sin is serious enough to be brought to the sacrament of penance. In some cases they almost sound as if they are embarrassed to take up the priest's time with what they perceive to be their minor moral failings!

A Higher Law

The problem with Catholics' adopting a minimalist approach to morality, whether in its rigorist or lax varieties, is that it stands in stark contradiction to the teaching of Jesus Christ and to the practice of the early Christian community. It is true that Jesus set himself apart from the Pharisees by eschewing moral *legalism*, but that does not mean that he endorsed moral *minimalism*.

In fact, Jesus handed on to his disciples a code of moral conduct that, far from being minimalist, was what we might call *maximalist*. In the Sermon on the Mount he repeatedly invoked the comparison between the Law of Moses and the stricter moral norms demanded by those who would enter the kingdom of God: "You have heard that it was said…" that you shall not kill or commit adultery or hate your neighbor, "but I say to you…" that you should not even be angry with your brother or look lustfully at a woman or hate even your enemies (see Matthew 5:21–44).

Jesus abrogates the Mosaic concession on divorce in the name of the original divine plan for faithful marriage between husband and wife (see Mark 10:2–12) and calls those of his followers "to whom it is given" to live the ideal of chastity for the sake of the kingdom of God (see Matthew 19:10–12). He sums up the whole of the Law and the prophets in the great commandment, "You shall love the Lord your God with all your heart, and with all your soul, and with all your mind, and with all your strength," and, "You shall love your neighbor as yourself" (Mark 12:30–31).

And as if loving one's neighbor to the same degree that one loves oneself is not hard enough, Jesus in John's Gospel raises the demand of love even further. In the Last Supper discourse he charges his disciples: "This is my commandment, that you love one another *as I have loved you*" (John 15:12, emphasis added). The perfect love that binds the eternal Son to the Father in the Holy Spirit in the mysterious interpenetration (*circumincession*) of the Blessed Trinity, the burning love of the Sacred Heart of Jesus for souls, this now becomes the standard by which Christian love is to be judged!

Pope John Paul II's great 1993 encyclical on fundamental morality, *Splendor Veritatis* ("The Splendor of Truth"), addressed specifically the danger of minimalism in Christian morality in a reflection on the Sermon on the Mount:

> *Jesus brings God's commandments to fulfilment,* particularly the commandment of love of neighbour, *by interiorizing their demands and by bringing out their fullest meaning.* Love of neighbour springs from *a loving heart* which, precisely because it loves, is ready to live out *the loftiest challenges.* Jesus shows that the commandments must not be understood as a minimum limit not to be gone beyond, but rather as a path involving a moral and spiritual journey towards perfection, at the heart of which is love (cf. Col 3:14). Thus the commandment "You shall not murder" becomes a call to an attentive love which protects and promotes the life of one's neighbour. The precept prohibiting adultery becomes an invitation to a pure way of looking at others, capable of respecting the spousal meaning of the body.[5]

For Christian morality, concluded the pope, *"Jesus…himself becomes a living and personal Law,* who invites people to follow him" by living his same commitment to total divine love in all its practical consequences, even when these are difficult or demand heroic virtue, as countless Christian martyrs bear witness.

So what does one say to the Catholic who does not know what sins to confess? Simply to examine his or her life against this maximum moral standard Jesus gives us. How fully do we live the Sermon on the Mount? Are we faithful to Jesus' intensified standards for observing the Law of Moses as it touches on our innermost thoughts and desires? How successful are we in loving God completely and above everything and loving our neighbor with the same burning love that flows from Jesus' divine heart? How truly have we subjugated the anxieties and concerns of daily life to the Lord's injunction to "strive first for the kingdom of God and his righteousness," confidently trusting that then "all these things will be given to you as well" (Matthew 6:33)?

To put it a bit more colloquially, as I like to do for a penitent who is having difficulty knowing what to confess: "Just tell me, what are the obstacles right now keeping you from getting closer to God? What in your life is preventing you from being fully one with Christ and his church?" This side of heaven, there is not one of us who can truthfully answer, "Nothing worth mentioning!"

"I'm a Good Person"

The third set of objections to approaching the sacrament of penance is the most serious because it is based in a moral mind-set that is the most dangerous. Some Catholics will say to the priest—sometimes even at the start of their confession—"Well, Father, I'm basically a good person, so I don't really have anything to confess," or, "I haven't really done anything wrong."

The humble acknowledgment of moral unworthiness before the throne of God's infinite goodness is the normative starting point not only for the sacrament of penance ("Bless me, Father, for I have sinned…") but also for the rite of baptism (the rejection of "Satan and all his works") and for the celebration of the Eucharist ("Before we celebrate these sacred mysteries, let us call to mind our sins…"). But the modern approach replaces the admission of sinfulness with what amounts to an affirmation of self-congratulation.

Clearly, this reverses the convicting sense of sin unambiguously attested to in the New Testament. Peter in the Gospel, seeing the sign of Jesus' divine power in the miraculous catch of fish, dropped to his knees and said, "'Go away from me, Lord, for I am a sinful man!'" (Luke 5:8). When the crowds of Jews in Jerusalem heard the first preaching of the gospel at Pentecost, "they were cut to the heart, and said to Peter and to the other apostles, 'Brothers, what should we do?'" to which Peter replied, "Repent, and be baptized every one of you in the name of Jesus Christ so that your sins may be forgiven" (Acts 2:37–38). John stated in his first letter, "If we say that we have not sinned, we make [God] a liar, and his word is not in us" (1 John 1:10).

And Paul, in his profound meditation on the moral struggle between "the spirit" and "the flesh" that occurs in the depths of the human soul, freely shared his own personal anguish: "For I know that nothing good dwells within me, that is, in my flesh. I can will what is right, but I cannot do it. For I do not do the good I want, but the evil I do not want is what I do. Now if I do what I do not want, it is no longer I that do it, but sin that dwells within me....Wretched man that I am! Who will rescue me from this body of death? Thanks be to God through Jesus Christ our Lord!" (Romans 7:18–20, 24–25).

Despite all these scriptural warrants, it is a popular view in contemporary religious culture that everyone is "basically a good person." In part this is a reaction against the rigorist Jansenist (Catholic) and Calvinist (Protestant) strains in early modern Christianity; in part it stems from the dogmatic and moral relativism of modern liberal Protestantism and the excessive optimism of some progressive trends in Catholicism after Vatican II (recall the effusive "creation spirituality" of theologian Matthew Fox); and in part it is influenced by the self-confident and upbeat tone in some of the Pentecostal, evangelical and charismatic Christian movements of the twentieth century. The result is that many contemporary Christians seem to have concluded that everyone —or everyone who "is sincere" or who has "accepted Jesus"—is fundamentally good. In this anthropological perspective, sin gets devalued to simple moral peccadilloes.

One sees this attitude clearly displayed in contemporary funeral liturgies, which sometimes seem closer to canonization ceremonies than to the traditional requiem Mass, in which the church commends the deceased to the mercy of God and prays for forgiveness and eternal rest for the person's soul. The change derives inevitably from the altered notion of the reality of sin: If everyone is really a good person, then so is the person who died, who must certainly be enjoying at this very moment the reward of the just in heaven. From such an anthropological starting point, two thousand years of Catholic piety devoted to praying fervently for the eternal rest of the faithful departed and offering Masses for the souls in purgatory suddenly becomes unintelligible.

Jesus' Imperative

There is, however, one glaring deficiency in the "I'm a good person" approach when adopted by Christians: Jesus never says in the Gospels to be a good person! Jesus tells his disciples, "Be perfect, therefore, as your heavenly Father is perfect" (Matthew 5:48). He teaches them the great commandment to "love the Lord your God with all your heart, and with all your soul, and with all your mind, and with all your strength" (Mark 12:30) and to "love one another as I have loved you" (John 15:12). He admonishes them: "If any want to become my followers, let them deny themselves and take up their cross and follow me. For those who want to save their life will lose it, and those who lose their life for my sake, and for the sake of the gospel, will save it" (Mark 8:34–35).

But Jesus never tells his followers to "just be good people" or "be nice to others" or "be responsible members of society" or any of the other moral platitudes that pass for wisdom in the civic culture—and in too many eminently forgettable church homilies as well.

For Christianity, morality is ultimately rooted not in ethical norms but in a theological imperative. Saint Peter sums it up well: "As he who called you is holy, be holy yourselves in all your conduct, for it is written, 'You shall be holy, for I am holy'" (1 Peter 1:15–16). The awesome human destiny revealed by the God-Man Jesus Christ is no less than our transformation into the very holiness and glory of God. And that demands a dramatic, radical and continual moral conversion.

The desert fathers—those first Christian monks who went off into the desert regions of Palestine, Syria and Egypt in the third and fourth centuries in order to follow the Christian call to holiness more completely—gave us a collection of pithy sayings and stories that convey profound insights into this quest for perfect union with God. One of them deals specifically with the distinction between "being good" and "seeking holiness" that we are discussing here:

> Abbot Lot came to Abbot Joseph and said: Father, according as I am able, I keep my little rule, and my little fast, my prayer, meditation and contemplative silence; and according as I am able I strive to cleanse my heart of thoughts: now what more should I do? The elder rose up in reply and stretched out his hands to heaven, and his fingers became like ten lamps of fire. He said: Why not be totally changed into fire?[6]

True Conversion

In the light of all this, one can readily imagine that responding to persons who do not believe they have any *need* to confess is much more difficult than counseling the persons who do not know *what* or *how* to confess. Should one read the former an examination of conscience, drawn from the Lord's words in the Gospels?

- "Have you loved the Lord your God with all your heart and soul and strength, and loved others as intensely as Christ loved you and laid down his life for you" (see Mark 12:30–31; John 15:12)?

- "Are you seeking first in your life God's kingdom and his righteousness—to be perfect in holiness—or are you preoccupied with the material concerns of this life, anxious about what you will eat and drink and wear" (see Matthew 5:48; 6:31-33)?

- "Are you losing your life for the sake of Jesus and the gospel, freely denying yourself and taking up your cross to follow him daily" (see Mark 8:34–35)?

Or should one cite the more practical examinations by which Jesus himself says souls will be judged in the end?

- "Are you angry and unreconciled with your brother or sister? Do you reduce human persons to objects of lust in thoughts and deeds? Do you take God's holy name in vain by swearing" (see Matthew 5:21–37)?

- "When Christ was hungry or naked or imprisoned or a stranger, in the least of his brothers and sisters, did you feed and clothe and visit and welcome him in them" (see Matthew 25:31–46)?

Or perhaps one should just ask if they are following that straightforward, simple but ultimately all-consuming exhortation that Jesus addresses to those who would be his disciples: "Have you made your priority in life following Jesus Christ, subjecting everything else—family, home, riches—to this one overriding goal" (see Matthew 19:20–29)?

Such an examination of conscience probably would not do much good. For what is missing in the hearts of those who protest they have nothing to confess is fundamentally the experience of *conversion*. I am speaking not of the initial moment of acceptance of faith in Christ (which in precise theological terms is referred to as "justification") but of the *ongoing conversion* to a deeper relationship with Christ and a more profound commitment to holiness that must accompany the Christian throughout his or her life (which theologically speaking is the call to "sanctification").

A beautiful scriptural text for this classic Catholic theme of ongoing sanctification is found in the third chapter of the Letter to the Philippians. There Paul states that "I have suffered the loss of all things, and I regard them as rubbish, in order that I may gain Christ" so as to achieve one end: "I want to know Christ and the power of his resurrection and the sharing of his sufferings by becoming like him in his death, if somehow I may attain the resurrection from the dead" (Philippians 3:8, 10–11). But then Paul immediately confesses that this is a goal still to be accomplished in his life: "Not that I have already obtained this or have already reached the goal; but I press on to make it my own, because Christ Jesus has made me his own. Beloved, I do not consider that I have made it my own; but this one thing I do: forgetting what lies behind and straining forward to what lies ahead, I press on toward the goal for the prize of the heavenly call of God in Christ Jesus" (Philippians 3:12–14).

The sacrament of penance, like the Mass and all the sacraments and the Scriptures and spiritual devotions and works of mercy, is a means of grace Christ has left us in his church. Christians who, like Saint Paul, are painfully aware of how far they still have to go in their spiritual journey eagerly embrace all these means. Motivated by the love of Christ, they are "straining forward" to the goal that lies before them of complete conversion and union with God.

CHAPTER FOUR

Why Do I Have to Confess My Sins to a Priest?

I n the preceding chapter we looked at some popular reasons why Catholics avoid the sacrament of penance. But we deliberately omitted one key objection to individual, private confession that is often cited by Protestants and even some Catholics: namely, why should one have to confess one's sins *to a priest*? Touching as it does on the core Catholic belief in the efficacy of the sacraments and the essential role the ordained priesthood plays in that, we want to consider this question in a separate chapter here.

I remember the first time I was directly confronted with this objection. As a young priest, I went to an office supply store to buy a new electric typewriter (still in use then!) and got into a conversation with the store owner, a pleasant young man who happened to be an evangelical Christian. Somehow the topic of the sacrament of penance came up, and he said to me with a smile, "I prefer to go to God direct."

Driving home, I mulled over this young man's comment. "Is it true that other Christians enjoy direct access to God's mercy, while we Catholics are burdened with the laborious sacramental machinery of confession?" I asked myself. "Are we priests some sort of spiritual interlopers in that most private encounter between a merciful God and a repentant sinner turning to him for forgiveness?"

At the very outset one can respond: If confession is an unnecessary obstacle and the priest an intrusive intermediary, then how does one explain the powerful *spiritual experiences* that so many Catholics testify receiving through the sacrament of penance? In the tiny, sleepy village of Ars in southern France, one can still see the confessional where, in the final years before he died in 1859, Saint John Vianney spent upward of sixteen hours daily hearing confessions. Thousands of people came there from all over the world, waiting patiently outside his church for days in order to have their time alone with the holy *curé*.

More recently a young American priest, making a retreat in Medjugorje a month after his ordination, was deeply moved by the experience of hearing pilgrims' confessions for four nights, beginning at 6 P.M. and lasting until 10 or 11 P.M. "I had known what it was like to feel the grace of the sacrament flowing *into* you when making a good confession," he said. "But now I had the incredible experience of grace flowing *through* me there in the confessional in Medjugorje."

Or as a student at Boys Town in Nebraska once put it more prosaically to his religion teacher, who had urged him to go to confession: "Thanks for encouraging me to do this, Sister; I feel like a whole load of garbage has been taken off my back!"

How does one explain these undeniable experiences by Catholics of a personal encounter with God's mercy and consolation, repeated time and again down through the centuries and across continents, when they confess their sins to a priest?

Not an Intermediary

For faithful Catholics, the explanation of the power of the sacrament of penance ultimately comes down to one simple, awesome truth of faith: When a penitent confesses his sins to a priest, he is really confessing them to Jesus Christ. It is Christ who hears him, Christ who absolves him and Christ who reconciles and consoles him. As the church has traditionally taught and the Second Vatican Council emphatically affirmed, the bishops, as successors of the apostles, and the priests who cooperate with them act *in persona Christi*, that is, "in the person of Christ," when they exercise their sacred ministry.

For example, in the foundational Dogmatic Constitution on the Church, *Lumen gentium*, the fathers of Vatican II define the role of bishops, whom they describe as possessing "the fullness of the priesthood," in these words: "In the bishops, therefore, who are assisted by the priests, the Lord Jesus Christ, the supreme high priest, is present in the midst of the faithful.… It is clear that by the imposition of hands and the words of consecration the grace of the Holy Spirit is thus conferred, *so that bishops, in an eminent and visible way, take the part of Christ himself, Teacher, Shepherd and Priest, and act in his person.*"[1]

And several paragraphs later, speaking of the order of presbyters or priests, who are the bishops' closest collaborators, it says:

> *Acting in the person of Christ* and proclaiming his mystery, they join the prayers of the faithful to the sacrifice of their head, and in the sacrifice of the Mass make present and apply the unique sacrifice of the New Testament until the coming of the Lord (see 1 Corinthians 11:26).… On behalf of the faithful who are penitent or sick, they exercise a

ministry of reconciliation and consolation in the highest degree, while they bear the needs and intercessions of the faithful to God the Father (see Hebrews 5:1–4).[2]

Nowhere is this power to act "in the person of Christ" more visible than in the sacrament of penance. There a weak human being, himself a sinner, dares to do what only God can do—forgive a person's sins—and even speaks the words of forgiveness in the first person: *"Ego te absolvo de peccatis tuis…,"* "I absolve you from your sins…" If the scribes and Pharisees were scandalized by Jesus' behavior in declaring to the paralyzed man that his sins were forgiven (for they said among themselves, "Who can forgive sins but God alone?" [Luke 5:21]), how much more understandable is it that non-Catholics and non-Christians, looking at priests who are ordinary, imperfect and sinful men, cannot accept their authority to absolve anyone of sin? Pope John Paul II, reflecting on this mystery in his apostolic exhortation *Reconciliatio et Paenitentia*, calls it one of the new covenant's "most awe-inspiring innovations":

> Now this power to "forgive sins" Jesus confers, through the Holy Spirit, upon ordinary men, themselves subject to the snare of sin, namely his Apostles: "Receive the Holy Spirit. Whose sins you shall forgive, they are forgiven; whose sins you shall retain, they are retained." This is one of the most awe-inspiring innovations of the Gospel!…
>
> Just as at the altar where he celebrates the Eucharist and just as in each one of the Sacraments, so the priest, as the minister of Penance, acts "in persona Christi." The Christ whom he makes present and who accomplishes the mystery of the forgiveness of sins is the Christ who appears as the *brother of man,* the merciful High Priest, faithful and compassionate.[3]

Icons of Mercy

The ability of the apostles and of their successors—that is, validly ordained bishops and priests—to forgive sins in the sacrament of penance is not an infringement on the rights of God but an amazing demonstration of the power of his mercy. God's love for man is so great, his desire for sinners to turn back to him and be saved so intense, that he grants this power of absolution and reconciliation to mere human beings. Thus the repentant sinner can have the assurance of hearing Christ say to him in a human voice: "Go, your sins are forgiven. Your faith has saved you." The returning Christian, like the Prodigal Son, can have the consolation of looking into a human face and feeling human arms embrace him, welcoming him back into full communion with God and his church.

For Sister Mary Kiely, an Irish Franciscan nun who has served in the United States for thirty years, the priest's role in the sacrament of penance as a living, tangible icon of God's mercy is paramount. She recalls vividly the experience she had going to confession as a girl of eight or nine during the parish mission at her local church in County Limerick: "I can still see that priest's face after all these years. He leaned toward me, listening to every word I said; he made me feel that I was the most important person in his world at that moment." She adds: "That confession had a profound impact on my life. For me, the profile of the face of that priest remains etched in my mind as the image of the mercy and forgiveness of God."

The synod of bishops gathered in Rome in 1983 to consider the theme of "Reconciliation and Penance in the Mission of the Church." There a Polish bishop spoke powerfully of the effect for an oppressed people living under the anonymity of a totalitarian, communist state to be personally addressed by the priest in the confessional as "you." Through the sacrament of penance, he said, Polish Catholics regained their human and Christian dignity as children of God. They heard the priest, speaking in the name and in the person of Christ, say to each one of them individually: "Through the ministry of the church may God give *you* pardon and peace. And I absolve *you* from your sins in the name of the Father, and of the Son and of the Holy Spirit."

In retrospect I see that the young evangelical owner of the office supply store did not understand the full extent of the Christian principle of the Incarnation. When the Son of God freely "emptied himself"—the Greek word *kenosis*—"taking the form of a slave, being born in human likeness" (Philippians 2:7), he showed that God's all-powerful love is so great that it can be fully present and operative even in what is "not God": created matter, mere human flesh, burdened down by the weight of sin. That is what happens when the Son of God becomes incarnate in the womb of a lowly daughter of Abraham. And it is also what happens, through the power of the Resurrection, Ascension and sending of the Holy Spirit, when Christ promises to be truly present in "his body, that is, the church" (Colossians 1:24) until he comes to judge the living and the dead.

The sacraments administered by Christ's priests are uniquely intense encounters—the crystallized concentrate, we might say—of this infallible presence of Christ in his church until the end of time. Jesus Christ remains, as the Letter to the Hebrews teaches, the one and eternal High Priest. The ordained priest, as minister of the church's sacraments, simply makes this spiritual presence sacramentally tangible and efficacious in this time and place as he acts *in persona Christi* to consecrate or absolve or baptize.

Strictly speaking, then, Catholics do not believe that in the sacrament of penance or in the sacrifice of the Mass the priest "takes the place of"—in the sense of *"replaces"*—the personal presence of Jesus Christ. If that were so, then the priest really could be accused of being a spiritual interloper, an intermediary who interposes himself between God and the Christian. No, the priest does not "take the place" of Christ; rather, he *"makes* a place" for Christ to act here and now in his church. Christ is always the one who is acting!

It is Christ, priest and victim, who is the one High Priest at every Mass, offering in an unbloody manner the eternal sacrifice of his Body and Blood, which he offered once and for all in a bloody manner on Calvary. It is Christ who is the one teacher and the Good Shepherd when, in the name of Christ, the bishops united with Peter's successor solemnly teach, lead and pastor the people of God. And it is Christ, as the forgiving father, who absolves the repentant sinner in the sacrament of penance and brings him back to life.

Mediators of Grace

It is for this reason—and not out of any clericalist exaltation of the priest's own person—that the Curé d'Ars, Saint John Vianney, penned his famous lines: "The priest continues the work of redemption on earth.... If one really understood the greatness of a priest, one would die, not of fear but of love."[4] Or as he put it simply: "The priesthood is the love of the heart of Jesus (*Le Sacerdoce, c'est l'amour du coeur de Jésus*)."[5]

When I visited his simple little rectory next to the church in the village of Ars, still maintained as it was in the middle of the nineteenth century, I saw another saying that Saint John Vianney wrote on the wall to the left of the entrance, so he would see it every time he went out to serve his people: "The priest stands between God and men like the glass that is between the light and our eyes." The holy *curé*, who could peer so penetratingly into the spiritual state of his penitents, also saw clearly into the soul of the priestly vocation: The priest is called to be transparent like a glass, so that Christ shines forth through him.

The life of Blessed Damien de Veuster, another inspiring nineteenth-century priest and pastor, illustrates this understanding of the priest's role perfectly. A Belgian missionary belonging to the Fathers of the Sacred Heart, Father Damien as a young priest visited the leper colony on the Hawaiian island of Molokai with his bishop. At the time it was rare for a priest to visit the quarantined island colony to say Mass and hear confessions. Catholics there had to do without the Eucharist, absolution and anointing throughout much of their lives and often at death.

On this particular visit the Catholic leper community begged the bishop to assign them their own pastor. Aldyth Morris dramatized this event in the 1976 stage play *Damien*, which was broadcast by Hawaii Public Television the following year. In Morris's reenactment the bishop replies that he cannot ask any priest to make this heroic sacrifice. At that Father Damien turns to the bishop and says: "They are right, Your Excellency. They must have one priest who belongs to them. To prove to them that God has not forgotten them.… You don't have to ask, Your Excellency. I want to be their priest. I beg to stay."[6]

Father Damien certainly knew how important it was to encounter the grace of Christ in the sacraments. When he himself was no longer allowed to leave the quarantined colony, he would row out from the shore in a small boat and shout his sins to a priest traveling aboard a passing ship, heedless of the embarrassment of being heard by other passengers, just so he could receive absolution. When he too contracted Hansen's disease, he mounted his pulpit at Sunday Mass and for the first time addressed his flock as "we lepers." Then all those in the church knew that in truth Christ had not abandoned them. Christ was there, consoling them and suffering with them and offering them salvation through the ministry of his leper priest.

As the French theologian Cardinal Henri de Lubac said so well, those called to serve as ordained ministers in the church are not *intermediaries* but *mediators*. Even then they "mediate" in a wholly secondary, derivative sense, because they make possible through the church's sacraments and its pastoral ministry Christ's own direct, immediate presence as the one and eternal mediator between God and man. In a work written soon after the Second Vatican Council, de Lubac explains:

> Those who are called to exercise this "pastoral" ministry have a share in the responsibility of Christ, the unique Mediator. They are the normally indispensable instruments, chosen to communicate the life of Christ and to maintain it within the Church....
>
> The word "mediator," sometimes applied to the clergy, should not be misinterpreted. Like the word leader, pastor or father, it is then obviously taken in an analogical or subordinate sense. And it does not mean "intermediary."[7]

Another great contemporary French theologian, Father Louis Bouyer, adds:

> The mediators, whoever they may be, in the perspective of the Gospel, beginning with Christ himself, and because all mediation is only an extension of his own, are never inter-

mediaries who persist in separating as much as they join.…
The lowliest among the faithful need the hierarchs of the
Church to receive the gifts of the Father,…but it is nevertheless *the* gift of God that the former receive, in which God
himself is given or rather *gives himself* in an ultimately
immediate way.[8]

There is a rather homespun analogy that I like to use to
explain this crucial difference between the priest as intermediary and the priest as mediator when I am speaking about
confession or any of the sacraments. I hand a kitchen knife to
a student or parishioner and say, "Try to poke the knife
through the wall."

"I can't," he protests quite sensibly, for the beams and
drywall are all in the way. But then I point to the electrical
outlet and suggest that he try inserting the knife there.

"No way!" he exclaims. "I'll get electrocuted!"

"Well," I respond, "the role of the church, and the role of
the priests who are its ministers, is to be like the electrical
outlet. The grace of the Holy Spirit is the electrical charge that
courses through all the power lines and circuits, accomplishing everything that is done in God's church. But to access that
indispensable charge, we need the lowly outlet!"

Too many Christians—non-Catholics and even some
Catholics—are under the false impression that the church and
its priests are like a wall, hiding God from his people, insulat-
ing them from the direct power of his grace. (And woe to us
priests and ministers if by our actions we lend credence to
this perception!) But in fact, the church and the priest are not
the wall; they are the outlet. You lay the exposed edge of your
soul in this outlet, and just like the bare point of the knife
pushed into a wall socket, you come into direct contact with
the full 120 volts of charge: the full force and fire of God's

Holy Spirit! This is what it means in Christ's church to be a mediator rather than an intermediary between God and his people.

Reconciled With the Church, Reconciled With Christ

How would our sincere evangelical friend respond to the above argument? Would it answer all his objections? Perhaps not. I could see his saying in response, "So you Catholics believe that baptized Christians can only have their sins forgiven by confessing them to a priest?" And the answer is no!

Just as the Catholic church teaches that one can be saved even without receiving sacramental baptism (see *Lumen gentium*, 14–16) or can enter into intimate communion with Christ without receiving the Eucharist (recall the traditional devotional practice of "spiritual communion"), so the church has always held that God in his mercy can and will forgive a sinner—even one guilty of mortal sin—who repents out of true sorrow for offending the God "who art all good and deserving of all my love." As the *Catechism* puts it: "When it arises from a love by which God is loved above all else, contrition is called 'perfect' (contrition of charity). Such contrition remits venial sins; it also obtains forgiveness of mortal sins if it includes the firm resolution to have recourse to sacramental confession as soon as possible."[9]

This is the reason why generations of Catholics learned the Act of Contrition by heart. Without a doubt many have said it fervently when faced with imminent death, whether heading into battle, aboard a sinking ship or lying in an emergency room. (I think a barometer of the failure of Catholic catechesis over the last forty years, both in Catholic schools and religious education programs, is that today few Catholic adults under fifty can recite any version of the Act of Contrition from memory.)

The theological principle at work here is that God is greater than the sacraments and other ordinary means of grace that he has established, and it is a pious intention to hope that through Christ, the one mediator between God and man, many souls are being saved beyond the visible confines of his church, even where the name of Christ is not explicitly known or professed.

But the complementary doctrine is also true: God has the power and the right to act with total sovereignty in how he wills to bestow his saving grace on human beings. God chose to reveal himself in this particular human being, Jesus Christ, and Christ chose to continue his mission in this tangible, historical Catholic church. That means that everything essential belonging to Christ and his church have lasting validity.

Christ's coming as the promised messiah of Israel, his two natures as God and man, the salvific universality of Christ's death on Calvary, his eternal high priesthood at the right hand of the Father, the divinely established church founded on Peter and the apostles which Christ united to himself as his own body and bride, the gospel and the sacraments that Christ confided to this same church—these are all now constitutive parts of the divine, providential plan that the church can neither alter nor dispense with but only gratefully receive and practice. Christ *could* have chosen some other way as the ordinary means to forgive serious sins after baptism, other than the sacrament of penance, but he didn't. Christ established this sacrament, and that is now definitive for his followers.

A sermon from one of the church fathers, the abbot Blessed Isaac of Stella, which is read yearly in the church's

Office of Readings, expresses this truth in a way that is admirably clear and sounds amazingly contemporary:

> The prerogative of receiving the confession of sin and the power to forgive sin are two things that belong properly to God alone.... Since only he has the power to forgive sins, it is to him that we must make our confession. But when the Almighty, the Most High, wedded a bride who was weak and of low estate, he made that maid-servant a queen. He took her from her place behind him, at his feet, and enthroned her at his side.... And as all that belongs to the Father belongs also to the Son because by nature they are one, so also the bridegroom gave all he had to the bride and he shared in all that was hers.
>
> ...Therefore, she too has the prerogative of receiving the confession of sin and the power to forgive sin, which is the reason for the command: *Go, show yourself to the priest.*
>
> The Church is incapable of forgiving any sin without Christ, and Christ is unwilling to forgive any sin without the Church. The Church cannot forgive the sin of one who has not repented, who has not been touched by Christ; Christ will not forgive the sin of one who despises the Church. *What God has joined together, man must not separate. This is a great mystery, but I understand it as referring to Christ and the Church.*[10]

Blessed Isaac had his finger on precisely the intuition that has lain at the basis of the church's penitential discipline since apostolic times. We can summarize it this way: *Reconciliation with Christ leads to reconciliation with the church; reconciliation with the church effects reconciliation with Christ.* If Christ is espoused to his church as intimately as a bridegroom is to his bride, then one cannot be a friend of Christ while estranged from his beloved spouse the church; for "Christ loved the church and gave himself up for her, in order to make her holy by cleansing her with the washing of water by the word, so as to present the church to himself in splendor, without a spot or wrinkle or anything of the kind—yes, so that she may be holy and without blemish" (Ephesians 5:25–27).

Saint Cyprian in the third century expressed the same sentiment: "But since…the generation and sanctification of baptism are with the Spouse of Christ alone,…*where and of whom and to whom was he born who is not a son of the Church so that anyone might have God for Father before he has the Church for Mother?"* [11] Being restored to health as a living member of the church necessarily reunites the sinner to Christ. He or she experiences once more the grace of Christ's Holy Spirit, just as that grace courses continuously throughout the whole living organism of the church, like the lifeblood that flows through and sustains a physical body.

The Community of Faith

Of course, it is perfectly appropriate to reflect on *why* Christ gave his apostles this authority to forgive sins in his name and "to bind and to loose" in heaven and on earth. That is the task of theology: to seek a deeper intellectual grasp of the faith that we profess, according to Saint Anselm's famous definition of theology as *fides quaerens intellectum* ("faith seeking understanding").

In the case of the obligation to confess serious sins to a priest, we have already mentioned one fundamental reason why Christ may have instituted this sacrament: God his Father wanted to continue *in a human, incarnational way* Christ's own forgiving presence in the world. He wanted sinners to hear a human voice, feel a human touch as they were reconciled to him, in the same way that Christ his Son had reconciled the suffering and alienated whom he encountered while walking the roads of Palestine. But there can be additional reasons as well.

One, it seems hard to doubt, has to do with this essential connection that we have just been considering between reconciliation with Christ's church and reconciliation with Christ himself, of being in communion with the church and possessing the Spirit of Christ. It is noteworthy that Vatican II chooses to cite a bold passage from Augustine on this very theme: "One possesses the Holy Spirit to the degree that one loves the Church of Christ."[12]

So in the sacrament of penance the priest acts *in persona Christi* but also *in nomine Ecclesiae,* that is, "in the name of the church." By the authority delegated to him by his bishop (technically called "faculties"), a priest in confession has the power to reunite a penitent with the community of faith from which he has been distanced or even cut off by his sins—the same community that he, as one of its members, has harmed by his sins. In other words, when a Catholic makes his Act of Contrition in the sacrament of penance, he is not only expressing his sorrow for his sins *through the priest* to God; he is also expressing his sorrow *to the priest* who stands there as the official representative of the church authorized to judge in its name. This is the "power of the keys," which Our Lord confided to the church in the person of Saint Peter when he said: "I will give you the keys of the kingdom of heaven, and whatever you bind on earth will be bound in heaven, and whatever you loose on earth will be loosed in heaven" (Matthew 16:19).

It is hard to imagine a more dramatic demonstration of the unwavering, rock-bottom Catholic belief that we are saved not as individuals but *as a community:* We are part of that community of salvation—variously referred to as the people of God, the gathering of all the elect and the communion of saints—that is really identified with Christ's very own body as the church. The *Catechism* does not shy away from underscoring this awesome truth that the "power of the keys" is inextricably linked to the very mystery of salvation in Christ: "The words *bind and loose* mean: whomever you exclude from your communion, will be excluded from communion with God; whomever you receive anew into your communion, God will welcome back into his. *Reconciliation with the Church is inseparable from reconciliation with God.*"[13]

This recalls the historical origin of the practice of penance in the first centuries. A Christian who was guilty of grave sins—traditionally considered to be murder, adultery and apostasy or idolatry—would approach his bishop to beg the forgiveness of the entire Christian community, to whom he would publicly confess his offense. In contrast to today's practice, in which the priest immediately gives absolution and then assigns a modest penance to be done later, in the early church the bishop would require the penitent to follow a strict penitential discipline, lasting at times for years, and only then restore him to full ecclesial communion and to active participation in the Mass and in the Eucharist.

Such a Christian belonged technically to what was called the "order of penitents," to which in the earliest period one could be admitted only once in a lifetime. The penitents would come to church with the community on Sundays, but they would stay in the rear and be unable to receive the Eucharist. They prayed earnestly for the day of their final reconciliation with the church, much like the order of catechumens who were undergoing the lengthy process of preparation for the sacraments of initiation.

One Latin rite priest was struck by a powerful reminder of this communal dimension of the sacrament of penance when he attended a Mass celebrated by a Ukrainian Catholic community in Russia. Before the liturgy began, the celebrant was hearing confessions to the side of the altar in front of the *iconostasis*. As penitents would go up to receive the sacrament, they would first *bow to the people*. This was a living sign, locked in the rich liturgical memory of the Eastern church's tradition, of the need to be forgiven by the Christian community when seeking absolution and reconciliation with Christ.

The Latin formula that was used by a confessor prior to Vatican II explicitly mentioned these ecclesial effects of the sacrament of penance. Before the priest uttered the essential words of absolution, "I absolve you from your sins," he said, "By its [the church's] authority I absolve you from every bond of excommunication and interdict, insofar as I am able and you are worthy." Thus it was made clear that the celebration of the sacrament of penance reconciled the sinner not only in the interior, spiritual realm of his relationship with Christ but also in the external, canonical realm of his status in the church. Even the most extreme ecclesiastical penalties of excommunication (being formally cut off from the living communion of Christ's body, the church) and interdict (being officially excluded from reception of the sacraments) could be removed, provided the bishop had given the priest the authority to do so and the penalties were not among those reserved to the Holy See.

Fifty years ago this would most frequently have occurred in the case of Catholics who incurred an automatic excommunication (*excommunicatio latae sententiae*) for remarrying outside the church after divorce—a particular law that was put into effect by the bishops of the United States in the hopes of shielding Catholics from the contagion of the divorce culture in this country (an effort that clearly failed, and so the bond of automatic excommunication was lifted in the 1970s). Today the most usual ecclesiastical penalty removed in confession is the automatic excommunication incurred by deliberately procuring or giving indispensable cooperation for an abortion (canon 1398). This law applies in the universal church for a similar reason of seeking to strengthen Catholics to resist the "culture of death," which is on the rise throughout contemporary society.

From Death to Life

Of course, reconciliation with the church refers to more than just the canonical effects of removing ecclesiastical penalties. After all, the greatest thing to be feared is falling into grave sin (or mortal sin), since this immediately deprives one of the life of grace and carries the threat of eternal punishment if one should die unrepentant. A Christian in the state of mortal sin still bears on his soul the indelible seal he received at baptism and may still juridically be considered a member of the church; but until he repents and is absolved of his sin, he exists as a "dead" member bereft of sanctifying grace, like a dead branch hanging listlessly on a vine. A Catholic in such a state cannot legitimately approach any of the sacraments except penance, since all the other sacraments (excluding baptism, obviously) can be received fruitfully only by one who is already spiritually "alive"—that is, in the state of grace. (Hence we have the traditional term "sacraments of the living" in contrast to penance and baptism as "sacraments of the dead.")

This is where sacramental confession plays its most critical role in the religious practice of Catholics: For those whose consciences perceive the presence of grave sin on their souls, it is the normal way to be reconciled with Christ and his church, in order to participate actively once more in the full ecclesial life of God's sacraments and grace. Concretely, that means most often that going to confession enables a Catholic who has fallen into serious sin to be able once more to receive the holy Eucharist at Mass.

A Spanish-speaking priest who has worked in urban parishes in New York City recounts that in his experience, poorer Hispanic Catholic communities seem to appreciate this link between penance and Eucharist. They know that to be readmitted to full communion with the sacramental Body of Christ at the altar requires first being restored to full communion with the ecclesial body of Christ by confessing one's sins to the church.

"You can't have one without the other, Eucharist without penance," he says. "That is why Hispanics especially will often approach a priest in the sacristy before or after Sunday Mass in order to go to confession—and why they cannot understand when an Anglo priest responds that confessions are heard only on Saturday afternoons or by appointment in the rectory!"

Some may criticize such eucharistic piety, pointing out that its emphasis on sin and guilt result in too few adults coming up for Communion at Mass. Where such is truly the situation, the priest should address the error pastorally.

We see the opposite error today, however, in many Catholic parishes. Ushers invite congregants row by row to come up for Communion, and just about everyone graciously obliges. One cannot help but wonder about all the Catholics in our society who regularly dismiss their obligation to worship God at Sunday Mass, those living with partners who are not their husbands or wives in the eyes of God, those guilty of domestic violence or sexual abuse or extramarital affairs and those in business or media or political life who publicly work to undermine critical moral values of God and his church. Too many contemporary Catholic churches appear to overlook the fact that one can be "in communion" with Christ in the sacraments only if one is first "in communion" with his church and with the moral law that it teaches authoritatively in the name of God.

God's Work

A second reason, it may be presumed, why God has chosen to link forgiveness of sins to the sacrament of penance is his desire to give assurance to sinners that, through their demonstrated remorse and firm purpose of amendment plus the priest's sacramental absolution and blessing, they are in fact forgiven and (in the case of serious sin) restored to the state of grace. I personally know of no more consoling words than to hear my confessor say over me: "And I absolve you from your sins." Assuming simply that, to the best of my ability, I have made a complete and sincere confession, then I have the certainty of being loosed from the guilt of my sins, according to the promise made by Our Lord himself to Saint Peter and all the apostles.

This absolution received in the sacrament of penance is a free gift of God's grace, the fruit of Christ's redemptive sacrifice on the cross. Therefore it occurs *ex opere operato* (literally, "by the work being worked"), to use the classic phrase from sacramental theology. What this means is simply that the forgiveness of sins in the sacrament of penance is not dependent upon the personal holiness of the priest giving the absolution nor upon how attentive he is to what I confess or how insightfully he responds with words of spiritual counsel. It is *God's* work, not man's, and God in his mercy has freely chosen to do this work whenever a validly ordained priest says the words of absolution over a sincere penitent to this end. So seriously does the Catholic church believe this that, according to canon law, any priest—even a laicized one, who has had all his priestly faculties and authority removed—can still validly and licitly absolve a sinner who approaches him "in danger of death" (canons 976, 986).

We Catholics perhaps too easily forget how difficult it is for a serious Christian to gain this same assurance and consolation through a purely private, subjective process. My Italian barber Louie—with whom I share some great religious discussions in the middle of haircuts—told me about attending a Bible study group in a nearby Lutheran church. The topic of confessing one's sins came up, and the minister explained the Protestant practice of acknowledging one's offenses in one's heart and asking the Lord privately for forgiveness.

A man in the group spoke up, relating how he had done just that on many occasions with regard to a habitual sin; but, he added with evident frustration, he never "felt cleansed" and in fact kept committing the same sin over and over. The minister responded sympathetically, suggesting that perhaps the environment chosen for his self-examination was not conducive to prayer, that he might consider looking for a quieter area in which to make his private confession. Louie said to me: "I've never gone to the sacrament of penance and *not* come out feeling cleansed. And at least for a while, it does indeed give me strength to avoid sinning again."

Saint Augustine, that expert in the discipline of acknowledging one's sins, adds another insight. At the beginning of Book 10 of his *Confessions*, Augustine reflects on the truth that

God knows a person's innermost self more deeply than a person knows himself. The confession of sins, then, is surely not for the sake of informing God of something he does not know! As Augustine puts it, "Whoever I may be, Lord, I lie exposed to your scrutiny."

There is a different motive at work in the sinner's acknowledgment of his offenses before God: namely, to bring one's sins into God's light and to allow his grace to enter the contrite soul to heal it. Augustine writes: "O Lord, the depths of a man's conscience lie exposed before your eyes. Could anything remain hidden in me, even though I did not want to confess it to you? In that case I would only be hiding you from myself, not myself from you. But now my sighs are sufficient evidence that I am displeased with myself; that you are my light and the source of my joy; that you are loved and desired."[14]

We human beings are masters in the art of self-deception and of hiding our faults from ourselves. By naming our sins to a priest, we put them out front, where both the church's minister and we ourselves must acknowledge them for what they are. And thus we can begin the process of remorse, of repentance and of opening up ourselves to God's mercy in hopes of conversion and a true transformation of our lives.

CHAPTER FIVE

Getting Back to Frequent Confession

So far, much of our discussion of the sacrament of penance has focused on its key role in the reconciliation of Christians whose consciences are burdened by serious sin. This is proper, since as the *Catechism* says, according to the law of the church "each of the faithful is bound by an obligation faithfully to confess serious sins at least once a year."[1]

But the *Catechism* immediately adds a strong endorsement of regular and frequent reception of the sacrament of penance, even for those who are not in a state of mortal sin: "Without being strictly necessary, confession of everyday faults (venial sins) is nevertheless strongly recommended by the Church. Indeed the regular confession of our venial sins helps us form our conscience, fight against evil tendencies, let ourselves be healed by Christ and progress in the life of the Spirit."[2]

What is the value of frequent use of the sacrament of penance? And why should the church be concerned that few Catholics avail themselves of it? That is the topic to which we turn now.

I have to admit at the beginning that I do not write as a disinterested commentator but as one who throughout his life has immensely appreciated the consolation and help provided by regular confession. My Jewish dentist, referring me once to an oral surgeon who was Catholic, confided to me, "He attends Mass every day," and added, "I don't know what he did so wrong that he feels bound to go to church daily to make reparation!"

Following the same line of thought, some readers may assume that my acknowledgment of having for a long period of time frequented the sacrament of penance on a regular basis must indicate some grave moral faults on my part that require atonement; and I certainly will not be the one to deny it. But in honesty I must state that it has not been out of an overwhelming sense of guilt or fear that I have become "hooked" on the practice of regular confession—though I do believe that a healthy dose of guilt and fear play their part, as they should for any Christian alert to the incalculable moral consequences of his actions and decisions.

No, in my life I have been strongly attracted by the mysterious experience of grace that I have found in this sacrament, by the real need I have felt for its strength and support in overcoming my recurrent faults and habitual sins and by the spiritual consolation and moral insight I have gained from the words of counsel shared with me by many wise and holy priest-confessors. Plus there is one other motivation, which grows stronger the older I get: I have the sense that the purification of self is a process that lasts all our lives and can even extend beyond our lives (in that mysterious but ultimately consoling reality called purgatory) and that attending to this task—which necessarily entails the penitential process of healing the wounds of sin—is a critical step on the journey to God. I will consider here each of these four elements that are inextricably bound up with the practice of regular confession.

A Mysterious Experience of Grace

I suppose I never developed an aversion to going to confession because from my youth the experience has always been enveloped for me in an aura of mystery and grace. I can remember my father taking me along every Saturday evening to confession at St. Mary's parish in Park Forest, Illinois—at that time one of the outermost suburbs on the south side of Chicago, just down the road from where the cornfields began. The recently built church would be dark and still, dimly lit by the flicker of candles and some subdued lighting.

After going to confession, the two of us would make the stations of the cross together, reciting our prayers as we slowly walked up and down the side aisles of the church. This no doubt contributed to a lasting conviction of the link between the sacrament of penance and the saving mystery of the Lord's cross.

The priest in the confessional was not some distant, anonymous figure behind a screen. St. Mary's was a small parish, and we all knew the priest in the confessional would be Father Henry Wilkening, the German pastor from Chicago who was its founder. On a warm summer evening my Dad would buy a cold soda and leave it on the table outside the confessional. Sometimes the grateful pastor, sweating in the closed box before the days of air-conditioned churches, would come out immediately to enjoy it. We would stay and chat with him for a while.

I realize not all Catholics share such fond memories about the sacrament of penance. Talking with many different people for this book, in fact, has reminded me that sincere Catholics still encounter in the confessional the brusque old pastor impatiently prodding them along, the tired middle-aged priest who acts as if he would rather be in the rectory watching the football game or the zealous young associate who is driven to deliver a moral harangue by a penitent's honest admission of sin.

Nor have I been exempt, I hasten to add, from less than inspiring confessional experiences—at times disappointing and on a couple of occasions troubling. And I am not even referring to my experience waiting for a flight in the San Antonio airport. I went up and asked a priest-traveler to hear my confession. When he came to the absolution, he could not remember the formula, so he just gave me a blessing. (If the plane had then gone down, would I have been absolved? I leave it to the sacramental theologians to debate!)

I do believe, however, that the worst response a faithful Catholic can make to a negative experience in confession is to stay away from the sacrament for the next thirty years. For if nothing else, the "boycott approach" denies oneself the opportunity to encounter many good and even holy priests in the sacrament of penance. These far outweigh the occasional bad or inept ones. And as mentioned in the previous chapter, the tremendously important teaching that the sacraments work *ex opere operato*, regardless of the talents or even sanctity of the priest involved, reminds us that in every instance where a sacrament is validly administered, God's grace is unfailingly present.

A personal experience as a young priest—the details of which must necessarily remain vague—drove this truth home to me in a powerful way. I was attending an international gathering of priests. For confessions the organizers had set up a long row of chairs, arranged in pairs, with a priest's stole at each station. I sat down in a chair, put on the stole and was soon joined by another young priest. He proceeded to sincerely confess to me a serious violation of one of the commandments. After giving him absolution, I then handed him the stole, he put it around his shoulders and he began to hear my confession.

Looking at him intently as he gave me words of counsel and then recited the formula of absolution, it suddenly struck me that this very human, sinful and repentant priest—he who a minute before was himself humbly begging forgiveness of God—was now for me the infallible instrument of God's infinite mercy and love. So was I for him, and so is every priest, I thought to myself. Deeply moved, I watched him lower his arm from the sacramental blessing, and instinctively I reached for his hand and kissed it. Then we went our separate ways, and I never saw this priest again.

Ongoing Conversion

On Ash Wednesday Catholics begin the penitential season of Lent by receiving the mark of ashes on their foreheads, while the priest or deacon says, "Turn away from sin and be faithful to the gospel." As any pastor can attest from the crowds that pack the churches even in the middle of the week, the distribution of ashes is one of the most popular devotions in the Catholic church. Perhaps this is because the observance of Lent prods us to renew our commitment to the Christian life. It reminds us that moral conversion is the work of a lifetime.

To be sure, the act of believing in Christ and receiving baptism—whether as a child or as an adult—effects in us a profound conversion. At that moment we are justified by Christ and begin to live as children of God through sanctifying grace. Still, justification is not yet salvation in glory, where we will see God face-to-face. The initial experience of conversion must be perfected through a lifelong process of "ongoing conversion," in which we learn how to die to self and to rise with Christ. For it surely takes a lifetime to complete the transformation that the author of the Letter to the Ephesians charges us with: "to put away your former way of life, your old self, corrupt and deluded by its lusts, and to be renewed in the spirit of your minds, and to clothe yourselves with the new self, created according to the likeness of God in true righteousness and holiness" (Ephesians 4:22–24).

This is where the sacrament of penance serves one of its major functions in the lives of ordinary Catholics: by providing a sacramental means, over the course of the months and the years, for regularly acknowledging one's habitual sins, for receiving God's grace in order to overcome them and for thereby drawing closer to God.

In a 2004 audience for priests and seminarians who were participating in a study course on questions of conscience, organized by the Tribunal of the Apostolic Penitentiary in Rome, Pope John Paul II said directly that "it would be an illusion to want to strive for holiness in accordance with the vocation that God has given to each one of us without frequently and fervently receiving this sacrament of conversion and sanctification."[3] The pope proceeded to outline the benefits of frequent confession. He referred to the three traditional steps of the Christian penitential journey according to the early church fathers, steps that were also followed by catechumens preparing during Lent for their baptism at Easter: the way of purification, enlightenment and communion.

The sacrament of penance by its very nature involves first of all a "purification" (the classical *via purgativa* or "purgative way"), commented the pope, "both in the acts of the penitent who lays bare his conscience out of the deep need to be forgiven and to be born to new life, and in the outpouring of sacramental grace that purifies and renews."

Secondly, the sacrament of penance is, said the pope, a "sacrament of enlightenment" (the *via illuminativa* or "illuminative way"): "Those who make frequent use of Confession and do so desiring to make progress know that in this sacrament, together with God's forgiveness and the grace of the Holy Spirit, they will receive a precious light for their journey towards perfection."

Finally, according to Pope John Paul II, regular recourse to the sacrament of penance leads one to a "unifying encounter with Christ" (the *via unitiva* or "unitive way"): "Gradually, from confession to confession, the believer experiences an ever deeper communion with the merciful Lord to the point of fully identifying with him, which comes with that perfect 'life in Christ' of which true holiness consists."[4]

Ongoing conversion to Christ demands a constant practical desire to grow in holiness. Saint Augustine outlines his analysis of the role of "holy desire" in his famous commentary on the First Letter of John:

> The entire life of a good Christian is in fact an exercise of holy desire. You do not yet see what you long for, but the very act of desiring prepares you, so that when he comes, you may see and be utterly satisfied....
>
> Such is our Christian life. By desiring heaven we exercise the powers of our soul. Now this exercise will be effective only to the extent that we free ourselves from desires leading to infatuation with this world.[5]

Staying on Course

In other words, as Augustine knew so well from his own experience, there is no static state in the spiritual life, no moral equivalent to "treading water." Whoever is not moving closer to God is thereby moving away from him. Aware of one's own human frailty and the effects of original sin, even the most sincere follower of Christ will experience a holy fear of being seduced by "the glamor of evil" (to use the wonderfully apt phrase from the rite of baptism) and losing the race.

Saint Paul himself said, "Run in such a way that you may win [the prize].… I do not run aimlessly, nor do I box as though beating the air; but I punish my body and enslave it, so that after proclaiming to others I myself should not be disqualified" (1 Corinthians 9:24, 26–27). Frequent confession provides the means for taking stock of one's moral life and for making sure one's spiritual compass is pointing squarely toward God—the really True, Beautiful and Good—and not some lesser, false pole of attraction.

Father John Bevins, pastor of Immaculate Conception Church in Waterbury, Connecticut, uses just such an image to encourage his parishioners to frequent the confessional. A twenty-three-year Navy chaplain, he recounts being aboard a ship where the officer on the bridge did not regularly check the navigational bearings—the sun line by day and the star line by night. The vessel drifted five degrees off course, a discrepancy that was hardly noticeable at the beginning. But going uncorrected, it ended up leading the ship's crew many miles away from its destination. In the same way, says Father Bevins to his congregation, frequent confession is how we regularly take our moral bearings to be sure that we are "on course" in the struggle "to eliminate vice and build up virtue."

In this parish the message preached is also the message practiced. Five days a week there are two priests sitting in the confessionals at Immaculate Conception Church for an hour at midday and an hour in the afternoon, with an additional half hour of confessions on three evenings a week. The word has gotten out that this imposing, beautiful church in the heart of this old, tired industrial city is a place where the sacrament of penance is nearly always available. Catholics from all over the region drive there for confession—several hundred penitents each week.

In summary, it is a serious mistake to minimize the moral significance of venial sins. The *Catechism* enumerates their negative consequences: "Venial sin weakens charity; it manifests a disordered affection for created goods; it impedes the soul's progress in the exercise of the virtues and the practice of the moral good; it merits temporal punishment. Deliberate and unrepented venial sin disposes us little by little to commit mortal sin."[6]

And then the *Catechism* quotes Saint Augustine. He acknowledges that in this life a Christian cannot help but have some venial or, as he calls them, "light" sins, but immediately warns against ignoring such sins on that account. "A number of light objects makes a great mass; a number of drops fills a river; a number of grains makes a heap," he writes, adding, "What then is our hope? Above all, confession."[7]

Confronting Scrupulosity

Some critics of frequent confession point out correctly that it can be abused. Such is sometimes the case with persons suffering from psychological neuroses and obsessions. A young man might knock at the rectory door at 10 P.M. to confess that he is troubled by impure thoughts. Or an elderly woman worries that she sinned by receiving Communion because the week before she missed Mass due to a blinding snowstorm!

But just as no public health official would dissuade citizens from frequently washing their hands simply because some people make an obsessive ritual out of hand-washing, so too no spiritual guide should dismiss the value of frequent confession just because some poor souls may use it incorrectly. In fact, I firmly believe that a profoundly healthy psychological insight undergirds the Catholic devotion of regular confession of venial sins. As Saint Thomas Aquinas noted, the human practice of both virtue and vice tends to become habitual. By our human nature made in God's image, we have a disposition to the good; but it takes constant exercise of virtuous acts for that disposition to become an acquired habit (or *habitus acquisitus*). The most important natural virtues thus acquired are classically called the "cardinal virtues": prudence, justice, temperance and fortitude.

By the same token, because original sin has radically flawed our good human nature, human beings also have a disposition toward evil acts done under the influence of concupiscence and base instincts. When it is these that are regularly repeated, then one acquires a habitual vice. The traditional list, enumerated by Saint John Cassian in the fourth century and quoted throughout the Middle Ages, are cited as the "deadly" or "capital" sins: pride, avarice, lust, envy, gluttony, anger, sloth (*acedia*) and—in an old tradition—dejection (*tristitia*).[8]

From a human psychological standpoint, frequent confession serves as an excellent means for drawing the strength needed to break these habitual cycles of sin, or vice, and to acquire the desired habits of virtue. Of course, deep-rooted, habitual vices are notoriously hard to eliminate. This is why those who avail themselves of the sacrament of penance regularly will often find themselves confessing the same sins. There is nothing wrong with that; the goal of the penitent in confession is not to strive for novelty!

Indeed, as Father Paul Check, a popular retreat master and teacher of moral theology, puts it, the more one comes to know personally the mercy of God, the more keenly developed becomes one's sense of sin and the more one wants to root out all its vestiges in one's life. For seven years Father Check has been giving conferences around the world to various congregations of women religious. When he hears their confessions, he notes how they go into detail on faults that others may find minor, or at least dull and repetitious. But this is a sign for them that they are refusing to "make peace" with their habitual moral faults and to abandon the effort to overcome them.

Father Paul encourages their resolve. He tells them: "When you see in the drugstore the Hallmark card that says, 'to err is human, to forgive is divine,' leave it on the shelf!" For to err by falling into sin is *not* human, he argues, even though it is a universal human experience due to the effects of original sin. It is contrary to what is human; it obstructs and degrades our humanity made in the image and likeness of God.

Those who confess their habitual failings regularly are not only looking back at the sins they committed in the past. They are also looking forward to how they want to live in the future, in accord with the divine image inscribed in the human nature, and they are drawing from this powerful sacrament its unique graces to fortify them for that struggle.

There is one final point to be made about recurrent patterns of sin: Habitual vices are usually *addictive* vices. Catholic spiritual tradition has a profound insight into the nature of such temptations when it refers to them as the "deadly sins." Why were they called deadly? They certainly are not the most abhorrent crimes, such as murder, torture, slavery, rape, deviant sexual acts, abortion and infanticide, genocide and persecution. The deadly sins are the attractive sins, the addictive sins.

In fact, on a certain level we *like* these sins: exalting our pride, satisfying our greed, giving in to envy and anger, feeding our many hungers and lusts and other appetites, even succumbing to the numbing paralysis of chronic dejection and spiritual sloth (the true meaning of *acedia*). And that is why these vices are so deadly. Like weeds choking the healthy vines, the deadly sins gradually suffocate the life of the virtues in a person and leave the soil fertile for grave moral offenses.

These deadly sins truly are addictive. And like all addictions, if we discover too late how much harm they are doing to us, then we realize to our alarm how powerless we are to rid ourselves of them. Thus, sooner or later, those who give free rein to one or more of the deadly sins end up becoming victims of these same sins. That is why a proper understanding of Christian moral teaching on habitual vice is not opposed to, but can actually be a valuable support for, the modern therapeutic response to the social epidemic of addictive behaviors.

Priests who are involved with twelve-step support groups, whether for alcoholics or drug abusers or compulsive gamblers, see how naturally Christian faith—and specifically, Mass and frequent confession—intersects with the approach pioneered by Alcoholics Anonymous. Making a painfully honest moral self-examination, acknowledging one's utter powerlessness to save oneself, confessing one's faults to the person one has harmed and asking forgiveness, turning to a higher spiritual power for the strength to be freed from the addiction, seeking the counsel of a wise mentor or sponsor, regularly drawing support and fresh resolve from a forum where failures and struggles are candidly articulated—the steps followed by a recovering alcoholic are the exact same steps taken in the moral life to overcome habitual sins through the sacrament of penance.

It leads one to think that perhaps the way to get across to contemporary Catholics the immense value, both moral and psychological, of frequenting the sacrament of confession is to borrow the more familiar terms from AA. Maybe we should be putting in our parish bulletins announcements for confession to this effect: "The weekly support group for recovering sinners meets in the church Saturdays from 3 to 4 P.M. Anonymity guaranteed. All those committed to seeking moral sobriety are welcome to attend!"

Moral Counsel and Spiritual Direction

In my experience one of the most beneficial fruits of frequent reception of the sacrament of penance has been the moral instruction and spiritual insight gained from the priests. What is the nature of this direction that a priest shares with a penitent after he or she confesses?

According to the rite of penance, "the priest should offer suitable counsel to help the penitent begin a new life and, where necessary, instruct him in the duties of the Christian way of life."[9] It is a part of the priest's teaching office that is, to my mind, unique. The priest gives his counsel in a forum that is formal and sacramental, yet his words are spontaneous, personal and not dictated by any rubrics. This is a kind of religious instruction different from preaching, teaching and the set exhortations contained in other liturgical rites. The closest parallel is the spiritual direction that priests, seminarians, religious and novices and many laypeople receive on a regular basis from a spiritual director, who is usually, though not always, a priest.

In fact, it has often struck me that the sacrament of penance may be called the "poor man's spiritual direction." Were even a minority of members of a parish congregation ever interested in seeing their priest every month for an hour's private spiritual direction, a pastor's schedule would be overwhelmed in no time. Yet every week for generations that is what countless fathers and mothers, elderly widows and young singles, had an opportunity to receive from their parish priests when, after their confession was finished, they could pause and whisper into the listening ear on the other side of the screen: "Father, do you mind if I ask you a question?" Having recently watched again Karl Malden's inspiring and realistic depiction of Father Barry ministering to his exploited parishioners laboring on the docks in the 1954 classic *On the Waterfront*, I could not help but wonder: How many poor, uneducated Catholic laity received the counsel they needed in order to persevere from a priest whom they learned to trust through weekly confession?

My mother does not hesitate to share the story of how a young associate pastor helped her get through a challenging period in her own faith life. She felt strongly that one of my siblings had been treated unfairly by someone representing the church, someone from whom she expected better. She found it impossible to swallow her bitterness and forgive this person. After talking out the whole affair with the young priest in confession, the image that really made an impression on her was the priest's concluding spiritual counsel: "After all, when Mary had to look up and see her son hanging there on the cross, don't you think she felt it was unfair too?"

Some years later the word got around the parish that this

priest, who had since moved to another church, had resigned from active ministry in order to marry. My mother refused to join in the local gossip among the older parishioners who remembered him, saying simply, "Father was there for me when I needed him."

Sometimes the spiritual direction that a priest is asked to give does not relate strictly speaking to "confessional matter"—meaning, sins that one needs to confess. When a penitent is carrying the weight of an emotional or physical burden that is also affecting his or her spiritual state (how could it not?), bringing it up to the priest in the sacrament of penance may be quite appropriate.

A young high school student, for instance, was devastated by the death of a friend in a car accident. His parents finally convinced him to go down to the church and talk in confession to the charismatic young priest who had just been assigned to the parish. The wise counsel and loving support that Father Tom offered him through that traumatic experience led to a real friendship. The youth would come down to the rectory regularly, sometimes with his high school buddies, to talk about religious topics. Father Tom became his regular confessor, spiritual director and confidant. A couple years after graduating from high school, the young man decided to enter the seminary.

Good Confessors

To a degree not necessarily the case with all the sacraments, a personally fruitful celebration of the sacrament of penance often depends heavily upon the maturity, the wisdom and the holiness of the priest who is administering it. In order to deliver meaningful words of counsel, the confessor needs the Spirit's gift of "discernment of spirits" (1 Corinthians 12:10).

The rite of penance defines this as "deep knowledge of God's action in the hearts of men," which is both "a gift of the Spirit as well as the fruit of charity."

In order to develop this gift, the rite admonishes the priest to prepare diligently for his role as confessor: "In order to fulfill his ministry properly and faithfully the confessor should understand the disorders of souls and apply the appropriate remedies to them. He should fulfill his office of judge wisely and should acquire the knowledge and prudence necessary for this task by serious study, guided by the teaching authority of the Church and especially by fervent prayer to God."[10]

I can honestly state that what has amazed me in my life as a Catholic is not the number of priests who do not measure up to this exacting standard but the number who do! I have been blessed with many wise, kind and holy priests whom I have sought out as regular confessors.

There was the rotund, rough-and-tumble priest in the Midwest high school seminary I attended for a few years, whom we called "Pa." In time he would leave a comfortable parish and go to Kentucky, where he has been pastoring a poor Appalachian community happily for over twenty-five years.

Some excellent Jesuits I met at college helped me to appropriate the intellectual depth of the faith: a wise philosophy teacher from the coal mining region of Pennsylvania, an idiosyncratic but brilliant English literature professor, a witty Boston Irish history instructor. In major seminary there was the diminutive, grandfatherly Italian Sulpician with the squeaky voice, who would always greet me with a big smile and a warm embrace.

Upon entering priestly ministry, I found myself turning to the great resource of retired and semi-retired priests, whose accumulated wisdom and pastoral experience are so often overlooked. One who had been a high school religion teacher for forty years told me how there would be daily lines of students to go to confession at his all-boys prep school back in the fifties. Then there was a monk who offered Mass in Latin with a Tennessee drawl while serving as chaplain for a nearby abbey of cloistered Benedictine nuns. I still see a former pastor, nearing ninety. He has me do a "sound check" with his hearing aid before we begin, but his mind and insight are as sharp as a bell. And a no-nonsense former military chaplain challenges me directly to confront my habitual faults (for which I always thank him).

Perhaps even more surprising are the many memorable encounters with priest-confessors whom I have met by chance. When I am traveling away from home, or maybe just driving to an appointment on a Saturday afternoon, I will sometimes slip into the back of a nearby church and anonymously go to confession (always identifying myself as a priest). I have approached priests for the sacrament of penance in sacristies and in rectories, in seminaries and retreat houses, in airports and in automobiles.

I have experienced powerful confessions at the Shrine of the Immaculate Conception in Washington, at the reconciliation chapel at Lourdes in France, and in St. Peter's Basilica in Rome. One might say that you would expect the church to exercise quality control in places such as these! But I can attest that I have been just as struck by the insightful words of priests in a tiny parish in northern New Hampshire, in a church outside of Mexico City and in a Dominican priory in downtown New Haven, which always leaves a side door open for any priest to slip in, ring a bell and have a friar come down to hear his confession.

It was in the last spot that I found myself on an overcast July day in 2003. The preceding twelve months of clerical scandal, accusations and vicious publicity had been a tortuous experience, especially for a priest like me whose full-time work was promoting the noble ideal of the priesthood to seminarians and young men considering a vocation. There in the confessional of the priory on Hillhouse Avenue across from Yale University, an old Dominican priest talked with me for half an hour.

Sitting in my car in front of St. Mary's Church afterward, I wrote down the moving words with which the friar concluded his counsel: "You do the work you do because you love God. You have a burning love for him. There is no other reason why you would be here, on your knees, confessing your sins and doubts honestly. And the Lord reciprocates your love. He loves you intensely. So you enjoy a special friendship with God. Try to savor that friendship. Pray for the grace of being able to experience more clearly this love that God has for you and you have for God."

I did not deserve such praise and kindness. But I believe that Christ the Good Shepherd *wanted* to console and support me in this way through that priest in the sacrament of penance. From experiences such as these I am convinced that every authentic encounter with the grace of confession can only lead in the end to thanksgiving and praise.

Healing the Wounds of Sin

There is a final motivation for frequenting the sacrament of penance, and it underscores the seriousness of the whole penitential dimension in the Christian life. With keen insight into the psychology of sin, the church teaches that there is a distinction between the *guilt* (*culpa*) of sin and what it calls the *temporal punishment* (*poena temporalis*) due to sin.

The guilt of all our sins, along with the eternal punishment of damnation merited by any mortal sins, is always forgiven in a sincere sacramental confession. But we would be deceiving ourselves—and ultimately trivializing the dramatic contest between good and evil, grace and sin, that dominates the history of our world and the history of our own lives—to think that after telling our sins to a priest, all is better and we can go back to living as if our sins never happened.

It is true that the gaping wound of sin is bound up in confession, but the scar often takes much longer to heal. The deadly fever has broken, but the process of recuperation to full health may be long and difficult. Herein lies the meaning of the penance that a confessor gives the penitent to perform and the whole notion of the need for "satisfaction" of the temporal punishment due to sin. As the *Catechism* puts it: "Absolution takes away sin, but it does not remedy all the disorders sin has caused. Raised up from sin, the sinner must still recover his full spiritual health by doing something more to make amends for the sin."[11]

Pope John Paul reflected on this need for reparation of the damage caused to others and to ourselves by our sins in his apostolic exhortation *Reconciliatio et Paenitentia*:

> Certainly [satisfaction] is not a price that one pays for the sin absolved and for the forgiveness obtained: no human price can match what is obtained, which is the fruit of Christ's Precious Blood. Acts of satisfaction...include the idea that the pardoned sinner is able to join his own physical and spiritual mortification—which has been sought after or at least accepted—to the Passion of Jesus who has obtained the forgiveness for him. They remind us that even after absolution there remains in the Christian a dark area,

due to the wound of sin, to the imperfection of love in repentance, to the weakening of the spiritual faculties. It is an area in which there still operates an infectious source of sin which must always be fought with mortification and penance.[12]

The pope here simply built upon the insight that Saint Augustine expressed with succinct clarity sixteen hundred years ago in his theological masterpiece *City of God*. Reflecting on the harmful effects of sin on human nature, he wrote: "Just consider the harm done by these wounds—the loss of integrity, of beauty, of health, of virtue, or of any other natural good which can be lost or lessened by sin or sickness.... *For there is no such thing as something wrong that does no harm.*"[13]

No one is more aware of this truth than women who are victims of abortion and those who work with them. That is what inspired Dr. Theresa Burke of King of Prussia, Pennsylvania, to found the international program called Rachel's Vineyard. This group now sponsors hundreds of weekend retreats yearly for women seeking healing of the spiritual and emotional wounds left by their abortion experience. A woman who is active in directing these retreat weekends, and who is herself a survivor of the trauma of abortion, describes the liberation that women feel when they encounter the forgiveness of Christ in the sacrament of penance.

"It's visually evident," she shared with me. "These women arrive Friday night scared, nervous, looking around to see if someone is going to condemn them. But when they have the experience on Saturday evening of going to confession to a priest whose attitude is like Christ's—loving, compassionate, forgiving—such a tremendous weight is lifted off them, because all along they had felt their sin was unforgivable."

But that does not mean the healing process is concluded. "The scar in the heart is so deep when we realize what we've done," this woman says, her sentence trailing off uncompleted. The experience of forgiveness in the sacrament of penance produces a profound catharsis. Like the sinful woman who burst into Simon's house in order to bathe Jesus' feet with her tears and dry them with her hair, these women can now let out all the sorrow and remorse they feel for their abortions.

They also begin to express their anger. "They feel cheated" because no one ever informed them of the consequences of having an abortion: the depression, the eating disorders, the dependency on drugs and alcohol. They begin to understand the church's teaching on abortion and are grateful for it, saying to priests and lay workers, "You've got to let the kids know what abortion will do to them, because no one ever told us."

Some will go on to become involved in programs like Rachel's Vineyard or WEBA (Women Exploited by Abortion) and the wider pro-life movement. Many of them will over time give back greatly to their church, becoming faithful Catholics active in their parishes. And yet this woman who has been working in the post-abortion healing ministry for years candidly admits, "The littlest thing can still trigger a painful reaction in me, even now."[14]

The courageous women of Rachel's Vineyard witness to the purifying experience that, in varying degrees, we all have to undergo in order to be healed of the tangible effects—the "temporal punishment"—caused by our sins. As the German Lutheran pastor and martyr under Nazism, Dietrich Bonhoeffer, wrote, "There is no cheap grace." True, grace is a free gift to us, but it cost nothing less than the blood and death of the Son of God on Calvary. And since no servant is greater than his master, we know that certainly in this life— and sometimes, also in that state of purification after this life called purgatory—we too, in the words of Saint Paul, must be "completing what is lacking in Christ's afflictions for the sake of his body, that is, the church" (Colossians 1:24).

Prayer and penance are integral parts of this purgative process by which we are healed of the effects of sin in our lives. So too are acts of charity and selfless commitment to others, especially through our fidelity to the vocation we have received from God. But especially effective for purifying and healing our souls are the graces obtained in the sacraments of the church: the weekly Eucharistic sacrifice, frequent reception of holy Communion and regular confession.

CHAPTER SIX

So Now You Are Ready for the Sacrament of Penance

I received a letter recently from a lifelong Catholic woman from the Midwest. She is now retired after an accomplished career in the food industry, where she rose to be food editor of a leading home journal. I had asked her to send me her thoughts on a lifetime of going to confession, but I was a little surprised at what she wrote:

> I've never found confession particularly easy. This in spite of the fact that for years I was at least a biweekly penitent.… Analyzing my tepid enthusiasm for entering that curtained box and revealing my sins to a person behind a veiled screen, I've concluded several things. We followed the rigid form: "Bless me, Father, for I have sinned.…" It all seemed so routine, so mechanical. The darkened box and the usually somber demeanor of the hushed voice behind the screen didn't frighten me, but made me uneasy.

She says that sometime after Vatican II she had the experience of going to confession face-to-face with a "brown-robed, barefoot-sandaled" Franciscan priest. At the time she was working in Minnesota and dealing with a troubling professional situation. She remembers clearly the experience of sharing her feelings with the friar.

"I was so helped by his words," she writes, "as he put his strong hand on mine and said: 'Don't ever forget: God may allow you to reach the cliff's edge, but he'll never let you fall over.'"

If you have read this book this far, you are probably like this woman in that you have decided you want the church in your life. And whether you are coming to the sacrament of penance for the first time or are returning from an extended absence, whether you grew up with positive experiences of going to confession or have only recently discovered the healing and support that this sacrament can give, you can probably benefit, as can all Catholics, from a review of the steps on how to receive this unique encounter with God's grace. That is the purpose of this present chapter.

Examination of Conscience

There are innumerable manuals printed intended to guide a penitent through a thorough examination of conscience so that they can recall their sins and make a good confession. By and large, I must admit that I find these not very helpful. Particularly uninspiring, in my opinion, are the canned "examination of conscience" reflections typically read from the pulpit during communal penance services. "Have I failed in my duty to love God and neighbor?" the priest solemnly intones. "Yesss," I think to myself, but where does such a general admission take me?

In fact, examining one's conscience is a quite personal exercise. It requires one to consider not some general questions about morality but the very specific question: In what ways have *I* been unfaithful to God? It necessitates examining, as the *Confiteor* recited at Mass puts it, the ways in which

I have sinned "in my thoughts and in my words, in what I have done and in what I have failed to do."

The examination has both an objective and a subjective component. Objectively, I must examine my conduct by the fixed measure of God's eternal law revealed in the Scriptures or discovered by human reason (the "natural law"), by Christ's word and his commandments that he enjoins on his disciples in the gospel (see John 13–15) and by the authoritative moral teaching of Christ's church, which enjoys the promised guidance of the Holy Spirit. In other words—let it be clearly said—acting on what I "feel" to be right and wrong is not sufficient for a faithful Christian!

Subjectively, as we already discussed in chapter three, I must be willing to judge my actions, not in comparison to others' actions or to some minimalist moral standard, but rather according to the perfect model of Christ's total love on Calvary and the "new commandment" he gives to his disciples: "Just as I have loved you, you also should love one another" (John 13:34). I must face the question honestly and forthrightly: Do I truly "love the Lord my God with all my heart, and with all my soul, and with all my mind, and with all my strength" (see Mark 12:30)? Or do I place "false gods"—security, pleasure, my own will—before him?

Examining one's conscience is a risky exercise, especially if its purpose is to prepare to confess to a priest in the sacrament of penance. There is a comfortable privacy about indulging in purely subjective ruminations concerning oneself. I can be as self-critical as I want as I sit alone in my room. But then the phone rings or I have to go out, and all those thoughts retreat to the far corners of my consciousness. When I have to face another person and name my faults out loud— exposing my dark, sinful side to the light—then my private thoughts are pulled out of the subjective realm and placed in the objective forum, albeit a confidential, "internal" one.

Now I have to look at my sins and talk about them *out there*, on the table, as another person is looking at them and talking about them as well. The risk is not so much what the other person will think of me as what *I* will think of me, as I hear myself owning my sins in front of another human being. Depending on one's state and vocation in life, here are some self-accusations that different individuals may acknowledge:

- "I make moral compromises at work to protect my job and get ahead."

- "I harbor an anger that I cannot get rid of toward my spouse, my parents, my adult children."

- "At night I go downstairs to the computer and log on to pornographic sites."

- "I am afflicted by illness or other trials, and I lose faith and trust in God."

- "Our whole life as a couple revolves around amassing material goods and enjoying ourselves."

- "Someone mocks or attacks the Catholic faith in the office or the club, and I say nothing."

- "I indulge adulterous, promiscuous or homosexual desires (actively or interiorly) that I have let take control of me."

- "I am not as loving, as responsible, as considerate a husband, a wife, a mother, a father, an employer or a worker, a priest or a religious, a single adult, as the Lord wants me to be."

The list could go on and on.

At this point readers may be saying to themselves, "Boy, an examination of conscience sounds like a lot of work!" Surprisingly, the answer is: It isn't. Usually five or ten minutes in prayer before going in to see the priest is a sufficient preparation for the sacrament of penance, but this assumes that one does not wait until the moment of confession to start examining one's conscience. Rather, a healthy degree of moral self-scrutiny should be a regular part of a Christian's daily life.

We have just noted that at the beginning of Mass—and indeed, most sacramental celebrations—the liturgy calls us to reflect on the reality of sin and to reject its hold on our lives. "Do you reject Satan and all his works and all his empty promises?" recites the priest or deacon in the traditional baptismal formula. In the same way, the age-old Catholic custom is to make a good examination of conscience at the end of the day, then pray the *Confiteor* or an Act of Contrition. By this means a follower of Christ is always checking his moral progress, expressing his sorrow to God for his daily failures and resolving "to do penance and to amend my life" on the coming day.

Were any of them interested in exploring it, sociological researchers would be surprised, I think, to find out how many Catholics still get down on their knees by the side of their bed at night and include some sort of examination of conscience and expression of sorrow for their sins as part of their night prayers. I carry the vivid memory from boyhood of looking down the hallway and seeing my parents kneeling on opposite sides of their double bed to pray and, I do not doubt, make a good Act of Contrition.

Some will say, of course, that a daily examination of conscience is the product of a typically Catholic focus on guilt, a neurotic tendency to "obsess" over sin. But that is not the point at all. Father Marty Heneghan, an Opus Dei priest whose ministry is devoted to spiritual direction and retreat work, recommends that an examination of conscience include three questions:

- How have I pleased God in what I have done today?

- How have I displeased him?

- How will I try to *improve* tomorrow?

The goal of any penitential discipline is always moral reform and spiritual conversion; otherwise it is just an exercise of wallowing in guilt, which can border on masochism. That is also the reason that an examination of conscience can usually be focused and precise. After all, the surgeon does not spend time doing an x-ray of the patient's foot if he is going to be operating on his gall bladder! So, too, a penitent becomes familiar with his own "moral physiognomy" and knows exactly where his chronic disorder tends to crop up.

The examination of conscience of a middle-aged celibate Catholic priest such as myself will no doubt differ, at least in material ways, from that of a college fraternity brother or a working mother with four children or a divorced business executive living in a condo. That does not say anything about relative states of holiness or sin. It simply recognizes that we each struggle with our own demons and therefore need to strengthen our moral defenses at different points.

It was in this vein that the Sulpician Fathers, the society of French clerics founded in the seventeenth century by

Father Jean-Jacques Olier and dedicated to the formation of future priests, would have their seminarians set time aside daily to make not just a general examination of conscience but also a *particular* examination of conscience. The purpose of this "particular examination" was to focus on one's primary moral failing and habitual fault—*le péché mignon* as they called it—which can be loosely translated as "typical weakness" or even "favorite sin." Father Olier and his followers wanted to make sure that their seminarians examined their conduct daily on their own specific point. This represented for each one his individual moral challenge, precisely because it was his characteristic fault.

Contrition and Firm Purpose of Amendment

It is not enough, of course, just to be aware of our sins. We must also truly be sorry for them and firmly intend, with the help of God's grace, to avoid them in the future. Sincere sorrow for one's sins is called contrition; determined resolve to reform one's life by rejecting sins is called a firm purpose of amendment.

As with the examination of conscience, so too contrition and firm purpose of amendment are fruits of a process that begins long before one sits down with the priest for the sacrament of penance. In fact, my experience as a confessor (and a penitent) is that the more one has wrestled with and felt remorse for one's sins, the more powerful is the experience of forgiveness when one finally approaches the sacrament for absolution.

It is like the story of the contrite woman in Luke's Gospel who bursts in on Jesus while he is dining at the home of the Pharisee Simon. To the shock of the guests, this woman, known to be a sinner, proceeds to kneel before Jesus, wash his feet with her tears and dry them with her hair. To Simon's dis-approving scowl the Lord gives a pointed response: "I entered your house; you gave me no water for my feet, but she has bathed my feet with her tears and dried them with her hair. You gave me no kiss, but from the time I came in she has not stopped kissing my feet.... Therefore, I tell you, her sins, which were many, have been forgiven; hence she has shown great love. But the one to whom little is forgiven, loves little" (Luke 7:44–45, 47).

The woman was truly contrite for her sins, many as they were. This contrition enabled her to open her heart in love to the Lord and receive his forgiveness. Simon, who did not provide even the minimum of hospitality to Jesus the teacher and prophet, had no contrition and so experienced little love and little forgiveness. Hardness of heart—whether in a remorseless, hardened sinner or in a complacent, self-satis-fied Pharisee (or Christian)—is the real block to true contri-tion. Before we even approach the sacrament of penance, the first conversion, therefore, must occur in the depths of our own heart.

It does not surprise me that Jesus was profoundly touched by the sinful woman's humble, contrite gesture. For what is most moving to us priests is when we encounter sim-ilar heartfelt sorrow in penitents coming to confession. I have met young men in stylish clothes who, driving past an open church on a Sunday morning, suddenly felt compelled to come in and open up about the emptiness of their lives, which were flush with money, drinking and girlfriends but devoid of love and commitment. I have listened to middle-aged hus-bands and fathers who have come down to the rectory on a weekend afternoon, torn apart over affairs they were involved in that were threatening to destroy their longtime marriages and families they love. I have bowed my head, lest even my glance make it harder for the words to come out, as tearful women confessed aborting their child years before.

Nor is deep sorrow limited to those bearing grave sins on their souls. I have witnessed moving experiences of reconciliation when a lonely, elderly widow admits that she has lost faith in God's love for her, overwhelmed as she is with grief and illness and sorrow. I have seen the pain of a young man who has taken hesitant steps into the gay subculture and recoiled in shame, confessing through tears that this is not who he is or who he wants to become. Or sometimes the remorse comes simply from longing for the closeness to God that the person knew years before and has now lost. A penitent misses the consolations and graces of the sacraments and especially the Eucharist, which he or she experienced growing up as a Catholic and later abandoned.

Real, heartfelt contrition is a grace. The fathers of the church referred to it as "compunction" or the "gift of tears," encouraging the early Christians to pray fervently for it. One important benefit of such a grace is that deep sorrow for sins makes it easier to form a firm purpose of amendment. Every confession, even if done on a regular basis and involving only venial sins, requires this sincere desire to amend one's life— that is, to break with the sins of one's past and to begin living the Christian life anew. Every celebration of penance is thus a moment of conversion.

Sometimes a priest is not even aware of the interior struggle that the penitent has gone through just to be with him at that moment in confession. One priest I know tells the story of being called one night to the hospital to do an emergency baptism of a sick newborn. After the baptism he was walking through the hospital lobby to return home when a man

117

approached him with a stunned look on his face.

"Are you a Catholic priest?" the man asked. He then went on to explain that he had been sitting there for a long while, wrestling with God and with his conscience. He knew he should go to confession, which he had not done in years, but he resisted. Finally, he made what he thought was a safe bargain with God. He prayed, "Lord, if you send me a priest right now, then I will confess my sins."

At that moment, he recounted in disbelief, the elevator door opened and this priest walked out! True to his word, he accepted the priest's offer to go over to a quiet corner of the hospital lobby and be reconciled to God through the sacrament of penance.

The pattern of interior moral struggle followed by a final surrender to God's grace has been repeated time and again throughout the history of Christianity. One of the most famous accounts is documented in Book 8 of Saint Augustine's classic *Confessions*. The brilliant, thirty-two-year-old rhetorician had been wrestling for years with a growing attraction to the truth and peace offered by the Christian life, and yet he still was drawn by the sensual delights he had known with his mistresses and common law wives since he was a young man in Carthage. The battle in his soul reached its climax one summer afternoon in a garden in Milan in 386:

> So, I was sick at heart and suffered excruciating torture, accusing myself with a bitterness that far exceeded the customary. I twisted and turned in my chains, until they could be completely broken, for I was now held but weakly by them, but still held....
>
> What held me were the trifles of trifles and vanities of vanities, my former mistresses, plucking softly at the garment of my flesh and whispering: "Do you send us away?" and: "From this moment unto eternity, we shall not be with

you," and: "From this moment unto eternity, this and that will not be permitted you."[1]

But then came the dramatic climax. Just as with the man in the hospital lobby, so too here it involved, if not exactly a miracle, at least a sign that seemed undeniably providential. While battling alone with his conscience and "weeping with the bitterest sorrow of my heart," Augustine heard a child's voice from a nearby house chanting: *"Tolle, lege! Tolle, lege!"* ("Take and read! Take and read!")

Immediately Augustine picked up a copy of Saint Paul's epistles that was at hand. His eyes fell on the words from Romans 13:13–14: "'Not in revelry and drunkenness, not in debauchery and wantonness, not in strife and jealousy; but put on the Lord Jesus Christ, and as for the flesh, take no thought for its lusts.' No further did I desire to read, nor was there need. Indeed, immediately with the termination of this sentence, all the darknesses of doubt were dispersed, as if by a light of peace flooding into my heart."[2]

The following Easter in the year 387 Augustine received baptism, the fundamental sacrament that washes away all sins and to which the sacrament of penance always refers. Thus was completed the second most influential conversion in the history of Christianity, surpassed only by that of Saint Paul.

Every break with sin is not this dramatic, of course, and every conferral of the sacrament of baptism or penance is not preceded by a wrenching, drawn-out interior struggle and a personally significant divine sign. But every conversion, every baptism and every confession do indeed require sincere contrition for one's sins, the authenticity of which is demonstrated in the firm resolve not to sin again. That is why the

Catechism says, "Among the penitent's acts contrition occupies first place."[3]

Confession of Sins and Receiving Absolution

This raises an important question, which needs to be considered now, as we turn to the confession of sins and the granting of absolution: Are there any situations in which the priest may *not* grant absolution to a sinner?

The answer, sadly, is yes, but this is determined not by the arbitrary decision of a confessor but rather by the free choice of the penitent. There is no unforgivable sin, but there are Christians who are not ready to ask for or to receive forgiveness.

The most common instance in which a validly ordained priest who possesses the proper faculties to hear confessions may not absolve a sinner is when a penitent reveals that, in effect, he or she is not truly penitent. That is, the person lacks sincere contrition, whether because of a lack of sorrow for sins, of intention to avoid these sins in the future or of willingness to do the penance and make satisfaction for the sins.

The Council of Trent emphasized the point in its Decree on the Sacrament of Penance precisely because of charges by Protestant reformers that the Catholic church made confession an automatic, grace-dispensing machine, regardless of the spiritual disposition of the penitent. In chapter four of the decree Trent taught:

> Contrition…consists in the sorrow of the soul and the detestation of the sin committed, together with the resolve not to sin any more. This disposition *(motus)* of contrition was necessary at all times for the attainment of the remission of sins…. Therefore the holy Council declares that this contrition implies not only cessation from sin and the

resolve and beginning of a new life, but also the hatred of the old according to the word: "Cast away from you all the transgressions which you have committed against me, and get yourselves a new heart and a new spirit" (Ez. 18:31).[4]

One of the most common, and also the most painful, examples of this situation is that of a Catholic who is divorced and remarried outside the church, or indeed one who is involved in any irregular union, such as living with a partner outside of marriage, being civilly married or living in an active homosexual relationship. In such cases the Catholic partner may not be admitted to penance or the Eucharist. Pope John Paul II said, in *Reconciliatio et Paenitentia*, that they "are prevented from doing so by their personal condition, which is not in harmony with the commitments freely undertaken before God and the Church" and which objectively contradicts the meaning of human sexuality and marriage in God's plan.

Pastorally these can be very painful situations, both for the person desiring the sacraments and for the priest, especially if the Catholic is actively involved in a parish and seeking to raise his or her children in the faith. The pope said that the church should always display "compassion and mercy" toward such persons and encourage them to seek God's grace by other means, such as "acts of piety apart from sacramental ones, a sincere effort to maintain contact with the Lord, attendance at Mass, and the frequent repetition of acts of faith, hope, charity and sorrow."

At the same time, the pope underscored the fact that pastoral concern cannot ignore the principle of "truth and consistency, whereby the Church does not agree to call good evil and evil good."[5] If all efforts fail to regularize an irregular union (by pursuing an annulment and then obtaining a valid marriage) or to rectify one that is radically flawed (such as

121

cohabitation outside of marriage), then the priest must challenge the Catholic to live a life of heroic virtue and sacrifice. He must counsel the person to end the relationship or, if this is morally impossible—as may be the case when children are involved—to live with the partner chastely by abstaining from sexual acts (what is called the "brother-sister relationship" or "internal forum solution").

If the individual is unwilling to do this, he or she may not receive absolution in confession or receive the Eucharist at Mass. For in such cases the person has not rejected—or at least made a sincere effort to reject—objectively immoral actions.

Given the extensive breakdown of marriage and the family in contemporary American society, a newly ordained priest may be reluctant to present the church's full teaching on these matters. In my priestly ministry, however, it is the laity who have taught me that they have a right to be challenged by that teaching—and that the church has a moral duty to proclaim and preserve it.

I remember, for example, the shock of being approached by a faithful parishioner after her daughter's confirmation Mass. Her former husband also attended. In a hurt, angry voice she asked, "Am I dead?"

"I beg your pardon?" I replied with a baffled stare.

She repeated, "Am I dead? Because if I'm not, how can it be that the husband who walked out on me and my daughter is free to come up for Holy Communion in our church, with his new wife beside him?"

That encounter brought home to me that the church too has a responsibility to remain faithful to the solemn commitment it witnesses when two people exchange wedding vows before God's altar, just as the abandoned spouse is called to remain faithful to his or her vows, often at great personal cost, by raising the children alone and not remarrying outside the church.

We also must not forget that a Catholic may *heed* the church's call to conversion when presented with the direct, uncompromising challenge of the gospel. If we really believe Augustine's statement that "there is no such thing as something wrong that does no harm,"[6] then it is a violation of charity as well as justice not to warn someone living in a state of sin to be converted.

A priest active in Hispanic ministry tells me that he knows of a number of couples in irregular unions who, often around age fifty or so, are willing to accept the challenge of living in total chastity—and going to another parish to avoid scandal, if the pastor asks them—because the sacraments are that important to them. "They appreciate that the Eucharist is something tremendous and holy, requiring one to be free of serious sin," he says. "And they are simply not willing to give that up—to give up being able to receive the Eucharist and go to confession in a Catholic church."

I remember a young couple wishing to get married who, not unlike many of their peers, had already started cohabiting. As I do in such situations, I explained the solid reasons for the church's teaching that the gift of sexuality should be saved until marriage, "in order that what we say with our body is not a lie, but is in accord with the commitment we have made in our hearts and expressed on our lips." I pointed out that contemporary social science verifies the wisdom of the Christian teaching, since couples who live together before marriage are much more likely to divorce after marriage, as well as to experience spousal abuse and a host of other problems.

I usually don't know if this pastoral admonition has any effect. But in this case at the wedding reception the bride came up to me (a very strong, independent woman, by the way) and said to me privately: "Father Chris, I just want you to know that my fiancé and I did what you said. We couldn't move out of the apartment, but for the last six months we've lived together as brother and sister because we wanted our marriage to be right."

After all has been said about the priest as healer and reconciler and spiritual director, it remains true that there is an awesome drama and power to what the priest does in confession. When a Catholic confesses his sins to a priest, and the priest as "the minister of divine justice as well as of mercy"[7] raises his arm to absolve the penitent, it is a reflection of the drama and power of the Last Judgment itself.

That is what a priest ordained sixty-five years shared with me recently. "The priest in confession is living the Last Judgment," he said. "It is a preview of what will occur at the end, when the Lord will appear and all deeds will be made known and he will separate the sheep from the goats."

His point was how important it is for the priest-confessor to judge rightly, conforming his words and his decisions completely to God's judgment and God's law. Similarly, the *Catechism* draws an analogy to the particular judgment at the moment of death in describing what happens in confession: "In this sacrament, the sinner, placing himself before the merciful judgment of God, *anticipates* in a certain way *the judgment* to which he will be subjected at the end of his earthly life."[8]

Reflecting on my own experience of giving and receiving absolution in confession, I can honestly say that I feel the transcendent mystery of God at those moments as truly as I do when celebrating Mass or kneeling in adoration before the Blessed Sacrament.

Performing the Penance

The last element of going to confession is receiving the penance from the priest, which one then performs as a way of making satisfaction for one's sins. As already explained in chapter five, it is a total misunderstanding of Catholic teaching to interpret the term *satisfaction* here in a sense that diminishes the eternal value of Christ's "once and for all" sacrifice to expiate sins on the cross. No, we are completely forgiven of our personal moral guilt by our contrition and the priest's absolution in the sacrament of penance, which draws its power from the inexhaustible treasury of merit won for us by Christ our redeemer.

But the harm that our sins do to others, to the church and to ourselves is real and substantial. So the priest who absolves us also assigns us some penance, whether in the form of prayer, sacrifice or work, that sets us on the road to healing these harmful effects brought about by our sins.

In some cases the kind of satisfaction called for by particular sins is self-evident from the simple demands of justice. For example, the priest in confession can legitimately seek a promise of restitution of stolen goods to their rightful owner or of compensation for injuries deliberately inflicted upon another, insofar as this can reasonably be done, as a condition for absolution (though the penitent is never required to reveal his identity to his victim or to turn himself in to civil authorities). In the same way, the priest may instruct the penitent to take concrete action to restore the reputation of someone slandered, especially if the slander involved a serious accusation that became publicly known and caused major damage to the individual.

Of course, the priest needs to exercise good prudence in any demands for restitution. If a teenager lifted some junk food from the local Walmart, there is no obligation to mail a check for $3.50 to the world headquarters of the multibillion-dollar corporation in Bentonville, Arkansas (though if the petty theft is habitual, it may be appropriate to suggest that the teen put the approximate monetary value of the goods taken into the collection basket at church or give it to some other charity). Similarly, one of the senior ladies who attends the monthly parish card party does not have to stand up at the next meeting and denounce herself as guilty of slander because she engaged in some gossip about another woman in the group!

More frequently the penance the priest assigns takes the form of some general spiritual exercise intended to assist a Catholic in reforming one's life and healing the wounds to the soul that are caused by sin. The *Catechism* cites as examples "prayer, an offering, works of mercy, service of neighbor, voluntary self-denial, sacrifices, and above all the patient acceptance of the cross we must bear," adding that the penance should "correspond as far as possible with the gravity and nature of the sins committed."[9]

Admittedly, we priests do not always show a great deal of creativity in this regard. Though I do not believe that the penance given in confession should be arduous or long—its goal is not to *complete* the penitent's spiritual conversion but simply to begin it—still a confessor should be able to come up with a spiritual prescription that at least sometimes goes beyond the old standby, "Say three Our Fathers and three Hail Marys" (something I admit assigning many times myself). A penance that to some degree is tailored to the penitent's specific situation is in keeping with the uniquely personal and flexible character of this sacrament, which we have been championing throughout this book.

It also accords with the instruction in the *Rite of Penance*: "The kind and extent of the satisfaction should be suited to the personal condition of each penitent so that each one may restore the order which he disturbed and through the corresponding remedy be cured of the sickness from which he suffered. Therefore, it is necessary that the act of penance really be a remedy for sin and a help to renewal of life."[10]

In my opinion this is most effectively done when the satisfaction for sin is *intrinsically related* to the nature of the desire that, in some disordered form, lies at the heart of the sin.

The church fathers seemed to have a natural grasp of the human "etiology" of sin—if we can borrow a medical term—which often eluded Christian commentators of the modern age, influenced by the strict moralism of Puritanism (in the Protestant tradition) and Jansenism (in the Catholic tradition). Augustine, for example, points out that sin does not consist of loving something that is absolutely bad (which is impossible) but in loving good things in a bad way. The sinner places the reflected, partial goodness of a created person or thing above the full, perfect goodness of God himself.

So in *City of God* Augustine states that greed is not wrong because gold is bad but because the greedy person desires it more than the justice that derives from God. Similarly, lust is not a defect in bodies created beautiful and pleasing by God; but it is a sin in those who let lustful desires take control of the soul, so that they are no longer capable of the temperance that frees one to desire the greater beauty of spiritual things.[11]

Saint Jerome sums it up magnificently in a letter he wrote in 384 to a young woman named Eustochium, who had embraced the consecrated religious life: "It is hard for the human soul not to love something, and our mind of necessity must be drawn to some sort of affection. Carnal love is overcome by spiritual love: desire is quenched by desire."[12]

I think that we priests in confession need to realize that simply urging people to avoid or suppress their evil desires is not enough—especially in today's world where "avoiding the near occasion of sin" in an absolute sense would demand that we all become hermits. Confessors must devote more attention to giving spiritual counsel and even assigning penances that help penitents counter sinful desires with holy desires, disordered love with authentic love.

Maybe we need to start giving penances such as urging affluent corporate executives to spend a Saturday morning volunteering in a house run by the Missionaries of Charity; telling strung-out working parents to find a way to "treat themselves" to a spiritual weekend retreat; and asking high school kids who are into partying and sex to visit elderly residents of a nursing home, where they may discover a different kind of beauty that resides in the soul. For only when one has experienced true spiritual joy, love and beauty is one able to resist their sinful counterfeits.

Such has always been the secret to the compelling witness of the saints. Saints Dominic and Francis revolutionized thirteenth-century Europe by showing the attraction of living in pursuit of truth and wisdom and following radical gospel poverty and peace. The Spanish saints Ignatius Loyola and Teresa of Avila reinvigorated the sixteenth-century Catholic church by being on fire with the love of God and the desire for saving souls, whether that led them and their followers on missionary adventures to the far ends of the globe or an "interior ascent" to mystical union with God. And arguably the most influential and admired woman of the latter half of the twentieth century was a tiny, bent Albanian nun who, amid all contemporary debates over social development and solidarity with the oppressed, revealed the true meaning of loving service to "the poorest of the poor": Blessed Teresa of Calcutta.

Saint Jerome had it right: "Desire is quenched by desire."

CHAPTER SEVEN

The Other Side of the Confessional

Alec Guinness, the renowned British actor, once was filming a movie in a village in Burgundy, France. He was playing the role of a priest. During a break from the shooting, he headed off the set, still in full clerical attire, to return to his room in the little hotel. As he was walking down the *rue*, a young boy came running up to him, calling out, *"Mon père!"* Guinness recounts in his memoir, *Blessings in Disguise*:

> My hand was seized by a boy of seven or eight, who clutched it tightly, swung it and kept up a non-stop prattle. He was full of excitement, hops, skips and jumps, but never let go of me. I didn't dare speak in case my excruciating French should scare him. Although I was a total stranger he obviously took me for a priest and so to be trusted. Suddenly with a *"Bon soir, mon père,"* and a hurried sideways sort of bow, he disappeared through a hole in a hedge. He had had a happy, reassuring walk home, and I was left with an odd calm sense of elation.[1]

Guinness recalls being struck at that moment by the mystery and power of the Catholic priesthood: that a young boy would feel such immediate trust and affection for him, a stranger and foreigner, simply because he believed him to be a priest. A year later Guinness entered the Catholic church.

Of course, in recounting his impressions, Alec Guinness was sharing simply what he felt while playing the role of a priest. But what are the thoughts and feelings of actual priests when they are sitting in a confessional, listening to sinners' heartfelt confessions, offering them counsel and absolving them of even the gravest sins?

It was interesting to me how many lay persons, when I told them about the project of this book, were most intrigued by that question. Are priests bothered by penitents' sometimes tedious recitation of their sins? Do they get bored hearing confessions? Are priests saddened that Catholics are not living more faithfully the moral standards of their faith? What is it really like to be on the other side of the confessional?

A Demanding Ministry

Pope John Paul described the role of confessor in the sacrament of penance as "undoubtedly the most difficult and sensitive, the most exhausting and demanding ministry of the priest, but also one of the most beautiful and consoling."[2] I would certainly say for myself that, compared with almost any other pastoral situation, hearing confessions requires the greatest attentiveness and concentration, the most care and prudence in how I respond. And after a few hours in the confessional without a break, yes, it can even at times become physically demanding. One particularly busy Holy Week I developed a crick in my neck from continuously bending my right ear toward the confessional screen; so I turned my chair around and leaned over with my left ear instead.

But like the pope, I have found my ministry in the sacrament of penance to be one of the most fulfilling and moving parts of my priesthood. I think and hope it is true that, except for situations where I had to leave to say Mass for a waiting congregation, I have never turned down a request by a penitent to go to confession.

There is nothing special about that. In the vast majority of cases in my life, both before and after I was ordained, I have never encountered a moment's hesitation by any priest whom I have asked to hear my own confession, no matter the time or the place. Indeed, a ninety-year-old priest once told me categorically: "In sixty-five years as a priest, I have never turned down a request to go to confession!"

Church law obliges a priest who is entrusted by his office with the "care of souls" (*cura animarum*) to provide for the hearing of confessions for the members of his flock "when they reasonably ask to be heard." And in case of "urgent necessity," canon law states, any confessor is obliged to hear the confessions of the Christian faithful.[3]

I believe we priests intuitively feel that administering this sacrament is, like celebrating the Eucharist, one of the most sacred privileges and important duties that we perform for our people. It is revealing, I think, that for all the abuses and faults that priests have been charged with throughout the long history of the church, I am not aware of any historical period when a major complaint against the clergy was that they violated the absolute confidentiality of the sacrament of penance. On the contrary, just as they have given their lives to celebrate and preserve the Eucharist, so too priests have gone to their deaths rather than reveal to demanding kings or imperious judges the secrets of a soul that they learned under the seal of the confessional.

Given the governmental animus toward religion in general and Christianity in particular in secular Western societies, it is conceivable that priests will again be called to witness to the inviolable sanctity of sacramental confession at the price of their own personal suffering. In some states, for instance, clergy are now included as "mandated reporters" of specific crimes such as child abuse, without any exemption for the absolute confidentiality of the priest/penitent relationship in the sacrament of penance.

Several years ago we even witnessed a state prosecutor secretly taping a prison confession made by a prison inmate suspected of murder. The confessor, a local pastor, knew nothing of the clandestine recording. The Oregon prosecutor only refrained from introducing the tape as evidence in court because of the strong condemnation by Bishop Kenneth Steiner of the Portland archdiocese and the ensuing public outcry.[4]

To begin to answer the question "What is it like to be on the other side of the confessional?" think of all the different sorts of people whom the priest encounters in the sacrament. The stressed-out mother feeling guilty about losing her temper with her husband and children. The high school student who has begun experimenting with alcohol or drugs or sex. The bachelor in his twenties or thirties who has not been to the sacraments in years but, perhaps at a wedding rehearsal, suddenly feels the need to go to confession. The middle-aged executive forced to reflect on all his adult moral decisions as he lies in a hospital bed the night before a serious surgery. The woman in her forties, crying over her abortion twenty years before, who desperately wants to hear that God—and her baby—forgive her. The elderly widows and widowers struggling with loneliness and jealousy and despair, who need to know that God has not forgotten them. Yes, even the little boy who expects to be taken very seriously as he solemnly relates how he disobeys his parents and fights with his siblings and teases his cat.

To the confessor there is some undefined trait that all these penitents share when they enter that sacred space, be it a confessional box or a reconciliation room or just the cubicle of a hospital bed. In that awesome meeting of a human being's freedom in admitting guilt and God's love poured out in forgiving grace, every Christian, young and old, comes to resemble the "little children" to whom the gospel promises the kingdom of heaven (Matthew 19:14).

Monsignor Lorenzo Albacete, a theologian and priest of the Archdiocese of Washington, made that point in a column about hearing confessions in *The New York Times Magazine*:

> Confession is not therapy, nor is it moral accounting. At its best, it is the affirmation that the ultimate truth of our interior life is our absolute poverty, our radical dependence, our unquenchable thirst, our desperate need to be loved....
>
> Confessing even the most dramatic struggles, I have found, people reach for the simplest language, that of a child before a world too confusing to understand. Silent wonder is the most natural response to a revelation that surpasses all words.[5]

A Humbling Work

What is it like for the priest to be part of this mysterious encounter, this revelation of God's grace and mercy "that surpasses all words"? Priests too are often reduced to "silent wonder" before the mystery of the sacrament of which they are the unworthy ministers. But sometimes they do articulate their feelings. When I asked several priests to reflect on their experience in hearing confessions, I was both interested and impressed by their sincere responses.

Firstly and fundamentally, the experience of hearing confessions *humbles* the priest. That was the almost universal reaction I received from the priests whom I queried. As one wise veteran pastor, himself a confessor and advisor to many other priests, put it: "Each time I say those great words, 'and I absolve you from your sins in the name of the Father and of the Son and the Holy Spirit'—and especially when I sense the penitent deeply receiving those words—I am moved spiritually and experience a grace of holy humility. I cannot express it well here, but it is profound to be saying those words and witnessing how they move the one receiving them."

It is indeed humbling to witness the sincerity and openness of Catholics—almost like that of a child—who unburden their consciences to the priest in the sacrament of penance, aware at some profound level that the person to whom they are really confessing is Jesus Christ. The priest cannot help but be inspired when he listens to a contrite fellow sinner willing to look humbly and honestly at his or her own moral failings and personal brokenness.

As a homilist I can certainly recall times when individuals have confronted me about things I have said from the pulpit. As vocation director I have had people argue with me about a particular judgment I have made. But as a confessor I have found it unusual to be challenged by a penitent about something I have said to him or her while administering the sacrament of penance. In fact, it is rare in my experience to encounter a penitent who even gives a sense of being guarded with me as the priest. The much more common situation for the confessor is to find himself looking into eyes that are keenly focused on his as he gives them words of counsel. Even through a screen I can sense when a penitent is attending carefully to every word I say.

Still more humbling for a priest is hearing a moral failing confessed that he himself is struggling with—and sometimes struggling with less conscientiously and successfully than the penitent. As one young priest describes it, "to hear confessions is especially humbling when the persons confessing appear to be more spiritually advanced than I am, and they possess insights about their own sinfulness which I have yet to recognize in my own life. I say to myself interiorly, 'Yes, I should confess that sin too.'"

For the priest it is like looking through a two-way mirror. He may find himself giving heartfelt advice to the penitent about dealing with a certain vice or difficulty, and to that person the priest appears simply to be reflecting the picture just described in the confession. The priest, however, is both looking into the soul of the penitent and simultaneously examining his own conscience; the words of counsel he delivers are addressed, as it were, both to the penitent and to himself.

This is not by any means to suggest that a priest is an effective confessor only when he has experienced the moral challenge and occasion of sin that is related to him in confession. That argument, sometimes used to question the capability of celibate priests to minister to parishioners with marriage problems, rests on a faulty premise that one would never think to apply to any other profession: as if a cancer patient should not trust an oncologist unless the doctor had been treated for a melanoma, or a defendant should not have confidence in a lawyer who had never been indicted and successfully beat the rap!

What it does reveal, though, is something of the ineffable wisdom of God's incarnational plan, which puts this wonderful sacrament of divine forgiveness in the hands of weak men who are fellow sinners in need of God's mercy. As the Dutch spiritual writer Henri Nouwen once put it, in a memorable phrase that became the title of one of his popular books, the pastoral minister always presents himself to his people as "the wounded healer."[6]

Meeting the Challenge

Along with this experience of being humbled, it is true that hearing confessions *challenges* the priest on many levels. Most obviously, he is challenged to listen attentively to what the penitent says, to discern the real state of the person's soul and to offer words of counsel that both console and motivate.

Sometimes what the penitent doesn't state is as important as what is explicitly stated. The mother who confesses losing her temper regularly with her family turns out, after a couple of brief questions by the priest, to be working full-time, raising four young children and also caring for a parent with Alzheimer's. A confessor may not be able to provide an "answer" that reduces the pressures in her life that give rise to the explosions of temper. But he can at least reassure her that her fidelity to her vocation as wife, mother and daughter is something of immense value in God's eyes, even with her faults. And he can encourage her to consciously offer that faithful witness, especially when she is worn thin and exhausted, as her particular "living sacrifice, holy and acceptable to God, which is your spiritual worship" (Romans 12:1).

At other times the confessor needs to interpret a vague reference, for instance, to "sins of impurity" or "stealing from work." Again, without prying into details unnecessarily or turning confession into an interrogation, the priest does need to find out if a penitent confessing impurity is talking about a lingering look at an erotic magazine cover in the check-out line or a nightly habit of accessing pornographic Web sites on the computer; whether "stealing from work" refers to occasionally pilfering some pens or notepads from the office supply cabinet or rather to stealing thousands of dollars from clients or taxpayers or investors through deliberate fraud.

In the sacrament of penance the priest is challenged to be concerned personally about the Christian kneeling or sitting before him. Pope John Paul II, in *Reconciliatio et Paenitentia,* said that the confessor shows his pastoral concern by "paternally admonishing these penitents with a firm, encouraging and friendly 'Do not sin again.'"[7] In other words, the confessional is not a "values-neutral" counseling center, nor does the priest seek to practice "non-directive" listening, as popularized by the psychologist and writer Carl Rogers in the sixties and seventies.

When I hear confessions of high school seniors who are already abusing alcohol and drugs or sexually acting out, I try to point out to them, in a way that is kind but also direct, that they are embarking on a path that will be inevitably self-destructive—personally, emotionally, physically, spiritually. When a middle-aged spouse shares with me thoughts about leaving a partner of twenty years and their children for a new, younger mate, I do not suggest "follow your heart" (as one counselor advised a husband I knew), but rather I do all I can to goad the person's conscience into considering the moral and personal consequences of an impulsive act that will violate God's law and permanently injure the lives of an entire family.

Real pastoral concern on the part of the priest does not end, though, with the spiritual advice that he gives to the penitent. The priest is also challenged to be a spiritual intercessor for members of the faithful who have entrusted themselves to him in that "sacred space where God is the third party present," to cite the wonderful phrase used by a priest I know to refer to confession. Minimally, the priest should do this, consciously and with conviction, whenever he recites the prayer of absolution over a penitent: "Through the ministry of the church, may God give you pardon and peace . . ." But ideally he should feel inspired outside of the confessional as well to remember and to pray—even to do penance—for those whom he has reconciled to Christ and his church.

The *Catechism* explicitly mentions this extended mediating role of the priest confessor, when it says that the confessor "must pray and do penance for his penitent, entrusting him to the Lord's mercy."[8] I admit that it is not a practice that, to my knowledge, many priests follow literally. But I am aware of a few cases in which a priest did consciously adopt this deeper sense of spiritual fatherhood and pastoral responsibility for souls.

One recently ordained priest, for example, relates how his godfather, with whom he was very close, was not actively practicing his faith. Every day as a priest and before that as a seminarian, he would say a *Memorare* before the statue of Our Lady for the intention of his godfather's return to the church. He had hoped that this would occur at his ordination—but it didn't.

On Wednesday of his first Holy Week as a priest, his godfather phoned and said, "I think it's time I go to confession. Can you help me?" The young priest finally saw the rewards of his long spiritual intercession as he gave Holy Communion to his godfather at his first Easter Mass.

A Source of Inspiration

Lastly, I believe that hearing confessions inevitably *inspires* the priest. This actually may be more the case now than prior to Vatican II. Father Benedict Groeschel notes in the introduction to this book that in the days of mass confessions every Saturday afternoon and evening, sheer numbers dictated that the priest's counsel to the penitent be kept short. He acknowledges a temptation for the priest to fall into a certain mechanical routine in the confessional, and as a result the long hours there could indeed become tedious.

Liturgical renewal has emphasized a more prayerful spirit of reflection in the rite of penance (for example, through readings from Scripture) and has encouraged spontaneous, personal interaction between confessor and penitent. This, along with the unfortunate phenomenon of reduced numbers of Catholics receiving the sacrament, may mean that priests today actually have improved as confessors and that the ministry of sacramental reconciliation has become more personally fulfilling to many priests.

Certainly, as a result of longer, less rushed confessions and more personal sharing between priest and penitent, there have been more opportunities for the priest to get to know penitents' spiritual states and to respond in ways tailored to their individual needs. One pastor described to me how this dialogue between priest and penitent in the sacrament of penance can improve his response as a confessor:

Personally I find that I become a better confessor, a better instrument of the Lord, when the person confessing manifests true faith in the power of the sacrament. This becomes obvious when he or she shows genuine contrition, and I sense that the person truly believes that this sacrament has the power to help him or her. Their confidence inspires me, and the Holy Spirit is better able to work through me in the advice that I give. It reminds me of the fact that our blessed Lord was better able to work miracles in the villages where the people manifested greater faith.

The reference here to the evangelist's comment that Jesus "could do no deed of power" in his hometown of Nazareth for "he was amazed at their unbelief" (Mark 6:5–6) is apt. When the Lord healed people in the Gospels, it normally occurred in the context of a personal encounter: Jesus truly "met" another person, dialogued with the person and then acted in response to the person's faith. It is no different for the priest administering spiritual healing in the sacrament of penance.

Priests are also inspired when they see the desire of their people for this sacrament and their gratitude to priests who make it readily available. One pastor of a large, busy Hispanic parish reports that he recently decided to forego saying good-bye to the people at the church door after celebrating Sunday liturgy and instead to announce before the final blessing that he would be sitting in the confessional after Mass for anyone who is interested. The response, he says, has been enthusiastic.

"People love it because the sacrament is there available for them." He adds, "I don't know how many confessions my associate and I hear on a weekly basis, but I tell you that I am grateful to God for this amazing sacrament, which not only helps transform the lives of my parishioners and my own but has also helped in the reshaping of the challenging community that I serve."

Finally, priests are inspired when they witness a deep remorse in penitents and a true desire to be freed from the "slavery of sin," to use Saint Paul's accurate phrase (see Romans 6). The humble sincerity with which a person fighting, say, sexual addiction or compulsive anger submits to the priest's spiritual direction, even when it may be challenging, touches a confessor. It moves him to want to assist the penitent in truly being liberated from the sin.

One priest told me, "What strikes me the most about hearing confessions is the number of people who are sincere in their desire to be close to God but who have fallen habitually into sins of weakness. Some have been struggling literally for decades with such things. God desires not only to forgive them but to set them free from this slavery."

This confessor's approach, borrowing a theme mentioned by Saint Alphonsus Liguori, is to urge such penitents to practice some moderate amount of fasting and mortification, in addition to their prayers and sacramental practice. "It does not need to be severe," this priest says, "but when this is added to the penitents' spiritual regimen, it has been my experience that they make steady progress in resisting temptation and are at last set free."

Whatever the specific pastoral advice given, a priest is as pleased to see a sinner at last overcome a habitual vice as a physician is to observe a patient making a complete cure from a long disease. If "there will be more joy in heaven over one sinner who repents than over ninety-nine righteous persons who need no repentance" (Luke 15:7), then that certainly also applies to a pastor of souls who is involved in the sinner's repentance in this life.

Becoming a "Confessing Church"
Hearing confessions humbles, challenges and inspires the priest. But the overriding sentiment that arises after a powerful confession is one of *praise*. As with all the sacraments, Christ established penance to be an intense, privileged experience of his saving grace and mercy. When a person—whether as penitent or priest—truly enters into the mystery of reconciliation with God and his church, which is ultimately

something God accomplishes rather than we, the only proper response is praise and acknowledgement of the greatness of God.

The traditional word, going back to the early church, for the fundamental act of Christian witness is *confession.* Those who suffered for the faith in the first Christian centuries through persecution or imprisonment or torture, but who did not die a martyr's death, were referred to as "confessors" of the faith. They gave testimony to Jesus Christ through both their words and their heroic sufferings.

There is thus a wonderful double sense to the word *confession* in relation to the sacrament of penance. On the obvious level, *confession* refers to the telling of one's sins to the priest as an integral part of the process of receiving absolution and forgiveness. But on a deeper level the word describes what is ultimately the goal and the only appropriate response for all faithful Christians who have experienced the gratuitous gift of God's grace and forgiveness of all their sins: praise and witness to the goodness of God. The psalm refrain that is an option for the dismissal in the rite of penance is "O give thanks to the Lord, for he is good; for his steadfast love endures forever" (Psalm 107:1).

The *Catechism* highlights this double meaning of the word *confession* where it talks about the different titles given to the sacrament of penance: "It is called the *sacrament of confession,* since the disclosure or confession of sins to a priest is an essential element of this sacrament. In a profound sense it is also a 'confession'—acknowledgement and praise—of the holiness of God and of his mercy toward sinful man."[9]

If we are to become a "confessing church" once again, we need to recover the truth behind both senses of the word. First, Catholics need to return to a regular, fervent practice of the sacrament of penance, confessing their sins to God through the person of the priest and receiving divine absolution and grace. If Christ willed to give his church a special sacrament of forgiveness and reconciliation, which like all the sacraments derives its efficacy directly from the fruits of Christ's sacrifice on the cross, then it is certain that he wants his followers to use it. A sinner who ignores a sacramental channel of grace established by Christ the redeemer is like the proverbial drowning man who turns down offers of rescue by a raft, a boat and a helicopter and then reproaches God when he drowns!

Second, Catholics need to recover a spirit of gratitude and praise for God's saving deeds in Christ. This will lead to confessing the wonders of the divine mercy by our words and by our lives. Another word for this is *evangelization.* To become a "confessing church" means becoming an evangelizing church, eager to spread the Good News of Jesus Christ in the twilight of the postmodern world.

These two senses of *confessing* are closely related. In order to become a church that regularly confesses its sins, Catholics must re-experience—or perhaps experience for the first time—a real, personal encounter with the reconciling grace of Jesus Christ the Good Shepherd. This experience is what all Christian efforts at evangelization seek to bring about.

And in order to become an evangelizing church that confesses Jesus Christ in today's world, Catholics need to draw on the particular grace that is the gift of the sacrament of penance. For confession and forgiveness of sins lead to the discovery of authentic moral freedom, moral freedom enables one to find real Christian joy and that joy is the inner source of the desire to spread the Good News of Jesus Christ, which is evangelization.

Becoming a "confessing church" once again is not, then, merely about increasing the headcount for Saturday afternoon confessions. It is about accomplishing the chief priority for the church in our day: the "new evangelization" and re-evangelization of the contemporary world. That immense project will not succeed without a profound spiritual renewal of the entire church, and such a renewal must be grounded in a return to the fervent celebration of all the sacraments, including the sacrament of penance.

A Model for Priests

We began this book with the story of an alienated widower whose encounter with a New England pastor in the sacrament of penance reestablished a bond with Christ and the church. We will end with the story of a Vietnam Marine chaplain whose work of reconciliation, through confession and through his whole priestly ministry, brought Christ and the church to courageous young men facing death.

Father Vince Capodanno's infantry regiment affectionately dubbed him "the Grunt Padre" because he would fearlessly make his rounds in the field in order to bring the sacraments and a consoling presence to his men, even when they were stationed in the most endangered front-line units. Father Vince was involved in six combat operations, and he was decorated with the Navy Bronze star and posthumously with the Purple Heart and the Congressional Medal of Honor.[10]

In the summer of 1967 Father Vince was serving with the Third Battalion of the Fifth Marine Regiment in the Que Son Valley, one of the fiercest combat zones in Vietnam. On the morning of Labor Day, September 4, members of his regiment came under a withering assault by a much larger enemy force near the village of Dong Son. Father Vince immediately requested permission to join two companies of the Third Battalion who were being flown into the combat zone.

After the helicopter landed, the chaplain gave general absolution and distributed Communion to all the men who sought them. When his company later ran into a fierce ambush, he left the relative safety of the command post and raced through an open area raked with enemy fire in order to minister to a trapped platoon who were in imminent danger of being overrun. According to an account written later by Lieutenant Joseph Pilon, a Navy doctor assigned to the same battalion, Father Vince, who had already been hit twice and whose right arm was "in shreds hanging from his side," was

> moving slowly from wounded to dead to wounded using his left arm to support his right as he gave absolution or last rites, when he suddenly spied a corpsman get knocked down by the burst of an automatic weapon.
>
> The corpsman was shot in the leg and couldn't move and understandably panicked. Fr. C. ran out to him and positioned himself between the injured boy and the automatic weapon. Suddenly, the weapon opened up again and this time riddled Fr. C. from the back of his head to the base of his spine.[11]

Father Vince's heroism lay not just in the fact that he so frequently put his own life in jeopardy in order that young Catholic Marines facing death could receive the sacraments of penance and anointing of the sick. Scores of soldiers, from privates to colonels, testified that the Grunt Padre ministered compassionately to men of all denominations without distinction. He bandaged their wounds, prayed with them and consoled them with words such as "Jesus is the truth and the life" and "Jesus said, 'Have faith.'" In fact, the second time he was wounded on that afternoon near Dong Son came while running under fire to a Russian Orthodox sergeant, with whom he prayed the Our Father and stayed for five minutes until the sergeant died.

To my mind, Father Vince Capodanno is an exemplary witness to the value and importance of the church's sacrament of reconciliation. But he is also an outstanding model of the church's entire ministry of reconciliation, which is lived out in unique and complementary ways by ordained priests and by all the members of the body of Christ. In the Grunt Padre many weary and frightened young Marines were able to look into the compassionate, consoling face of Jesus the Good Shepherd, he who goes in search of the lost sheep and then places it on his own shoulders to bring it home.

The Navy doctor referred to that famous parable of the Good Shepherd (see Luke 15) after the chaplain's death, in order to describe Father Vince's special way of ministering to the men in his care. He would not stay safely sheltered on a large base or a command headquarters but would at every opportunity head out into the field, to the "hot zones" and lonely outposts, where the men most in need were to be found. Lieutenant Pilon writes: "His audience was always a small group of 20 to 40 Marines gathered together on a hillside, or behind some rocks, hearing confessions—saying Mass. It was almost as though he had decided to leave the 'other 99' in a safe area and go after the one who had gotten in trouble."[12]

Another striking observation comes from Marine Corporal George Phillips. He recalled that when Father Vince approached men who were wounded, he was "determined to do what he was there to do.... He would not get down because he wanted to look at them straight in the eyes. People were yelling at him 'Father, get down.' Guys were getting machine-gunned lying on the ground. But Father Capodanno wanted to calm the wounded by looking them in the eyes."[13]

This last comment prompts one final personal observation about celebrating the sacrament of penance. I have been very moved at times both in receiving and in administering the sacrament of penance behind the anonymity of a screen. But I believe that my most powerful confessions, whether as a penitent or as a priest, have occurred when I celebrated the sacrament face to face. Perhaps the corporal's note about the pastoral practice of the Grunt Padre to "look at the wounded straight in the eyes" provides the explanation for what I have experienced in my own life and priestly ministry. By the mystery of the sacrament of penance, through the mediation of a weak fellow sinner, a guilty and suffering human being gets the incredible gift of being able to look directly into the forgiving, consoling and infinitely loving eyes of Jesus Christ. Spiritually, the meeting always takes place face to face.

He who is the Good Shepherd left us this beautiful sacrament of reconciliation as the concrete way that he searches still today for the one lost sheep. Finding it, he places it on his shoulders and brings it back to the safety of the flock. Once Catholics realize that it is just this kind of powerful and holy encounter with Jesus Christ that awaits them whenever a priest sits quietly, unobtrusively in a confessional or reconciliation room, then we will surely become more fully and in both senses of the word a "confessing church."

Notes

Chapter One: Whatever Happened to the Sacrament of Penance?

1. John Paul II, *Crossing the Threshold of Hope*, Vittorio Messori, ed. (New York: Knopf, 1994), p. 223.

2. Henri de Lubac, *At the Service of the Church: Henri de Lubac Reflects on the Circumstances That Occasioned His Writings*, Anne Elizabeth Englund, trans. (San Francisco: Ignatius, 1993), p. 172.

3. Pope John Paul II, *Redemptoris Missio*, n. 3 in *The Encyclicals of John Paul II*, J. Michael Miller, ed. (Huntington, Ind.: Our Sunday Visitor, 1996), p. 496.

Chapter Two: The Sacrament for Contemporary Catholics

1. Rite of Penance, n. 10, in *The Rites of the Catholic Church as Revised by Decree of the Second Vatican Ecumenical Council and Published by Authority of Pope Paul VI*, study edition (New York: Pueblo, 1983), p. 368.

2. *Catechism of the Catholic Church Revised in Accordance with the Official Latin Text Promulgated by Pope John Paul II*, second edition (Washington: United States Catholic Conference; Libreria Editrice Vaticana, 1997), n. 1497: p. 374.

3. All references to church canons come from *Code of Canon Law*, Latin-English Edition (Washington: Canon Law Society of America, 1983).

4. Tertullian, *De Paenitentia* 4, 2, found in Migne, *Patrologia Latina* 1, 1343; cited in *Catechism*, n. 1446, p. 363.

5. Friedrich Nietzsche, *The Joyful Wisdom (La Gaya Scienza)*, Thomas Common, trans., in *The Complete Works of Friedrich Nietzsche*, vol. 10 (London: T. N. Foulis, 1910), p. 313.

6. *Catechism*, n. 1466, p. 368.
7. *Catechism*, n. 1466, p. 368.
8. *September 11, 2001: We Were There…Catholic Priests and How They Responded in Their Own Words,* Secretariat for Vocations and Priestly Formation, ed. (Washington: United States Conference of Catholic Bishops, 2003), p. 2.

Chapter Three: Popular Reasons for Avoiding Confession (and Why They Are Wrong)

1. Council of Trent, *Decree on the Doctrine of the Sacrament of Penance*, chap. 5: "On Confession," cited in Henricus Denzinger and Adolfus Schönmetzer, *Enchiridion Symbolorum, Definitionum et Declarationum de rebus fidei et morum,* 36th edition, (Freiburg: Herder, 1976), n. 1679.
2. Saint Jerome, *Commentary on Ecclesiastes*, 10, 11, in Migne, *Patrologia Latina,* 23, 1096; cited in Denzinger and Schönmetzer, n. 1680, and *Catechism of the Catholic Church*, n. 1456, p. 365.
3. Pope John Paul II, *Reconciliatio et Paenitentia*, Post-Synodal Apostolic Exhortation on Reconciliation and Penance in the Mission of the Church Today (Rome, 1984), nn. 5–6 (Boston: St. Paul), pp. 22–23.
4. From a personal audiotape of a meeting that took place at the White House with President Bill Clinton and a group of about twenty-five editors of U.S. Catholic newspapers, including myself; Washington, D.C., September 15, 1995.
5. Pope John Paul II, *Veritatis Splendor* ("The Splendor of Truth"), Encyclical Letter Regarding Certain Fundamental Questions of the Church's Moral Teachings (Rome, 1993), n. 15; (Washington: United States Catholic Conference, 1993), pp. 26–27.
6. *The Wisdom of the Desert: Sayings from the Desert Fathers of*

the Fourth Century, Thomas Merton, trans. (New York: New Directions, 1970), p. 50.

Chapter Four: Why Do I Have to Confess My Sins to a Priest?

1. *Lumen Gentium*, 21; my translation, emphasis added. In the original Latin text, the highlighted phrase ends with the words *"et in Eius persona agant."*
2. *Lumen Gentium*, 28; my translation, emphasis added. Here the highlighted phrase reads in the Latin: *"in persona Christi agentes."*
3. *Reconciliatio et Paenitentia*, n. 29, pp. 108–109.
4. Bernard Nodet, *The Heart of the Curé of Ars*, John Joyce, trans. (New York: Benziger Brothers, 1963), p. 77.
5. Quoted in Bernard Nodet, *Jean-Marie Vianney, Curé d'Ars: Sa Pensée, Son Coeur* (Paris: Edition Xavier Mappus, 1959), p. 100; cited in French in *Catéchisme de l'Église Catholique* (Paris: Mame/Plon; Vatican City: Librairie Editrice Vaticane, 1992), n. 1598, p. 339.
6. Aldyth Morris, *Damien* (Honolulu: University of Hawaii Press, 1990), p. 12.
7. Henri de Lubac, *The Motherhood of the Church, followed by Particular Churches in the Universal Church and an interview conducted by Gwendoline Jarczyk*, Sergia Englund, trans. (San Francisco: Ignatius, 1982), p. 93.
8. Louis Bouyer, *The Church of God: Body of Christ and Temple of the Holy Spirit*, Charles Underhill Quinn, trans. (Chicago: Franciscan Herald, 1982), pp. 259–260.
9. *Catechism*, n. 1452, p. 364.
10. Blessed Isaac of Stella, *Sermo 11*, found in Migne, *Patrologia Latina* 194, 1728–1729; cited in *The Office of Readings According to the Roman Rite*, International

Commission on English in the Liturgy, trans. (Boston: St. Paul, 1983) for Friday of the twenty-third week in Ordinary Time, pp. 1059–1060.

11. Cyprian, "Letter 74," n. 7; in Saint Cyprian, *Letters (1–81)*, Sister Rose Bernard Donna, trans., *The Fathers of the Church* series (Washington: Catholic University of America Press, 1964), p. 290, emphasis added.

12. Augustine, *Tractatus in evangelium Ioannis* 32, 8, in Migne, *Patrologia Latina* 35, 1646; cited in Vatican II, *Optatam Totius*, Decree on the Training of Priests, p. 9.

13. *Catechism*, n. 1445; p. 363.

14. Augustine, *Confessions*, Book 10, chap. 2, cited in *The Office of Readings*, Tuesday of the eighth week in Ordinary Time, p. 304.

Chapter Five: Getting Back to Frequent Confession

1. *Catechism*, n. 1457, p. 365; see *Code of Canon Law*, canon 989.

2. *Catechism*, n. 1458, p. 366.

3. Pope John Paul II, "Confessors carry the 'message of reconciliation,'" *L'Osservatore Romano*, English language edition, n. 14 (April 7, 2004), p. 8.

4. Pope John Paul II, "Confessors carry the 'message of reconciliation'.", p. 8.

5. Augustine, *Tractatus in epistolam Ioannis ad Parthos* 4; in Migne, *Patrologia Latina 35*, 2008–2009, cited in *The Office of Readings*, Friday of the sixth week in Ordinary Time, p. 272.

6. *Catechism*, n. 1863, p. 456.

7. Augustine, *Tractatus in epistolam Ioannis ad Parthos* 1, 6; in Migne, *Patrologia Latina* 35, 1982. See *Catechism*, n. 1863, p. 456.

8. *Catechism*, n. 1866, p. 457.

9. Rite of Penance, n. 14, in *The Rites of the Catholic Church*, p. 371.

10. Rite of Penance, n. 10, in *The Rites of the Catholic Church*, p. 368.

11. *Catechism*, n. 1459; p. 366.

12. *Reconciliatio et Paenitentia*, n. 31: pp. 123–124.

13. Augustine, *The City of God*, bk. 12, chap. 3; in Saint Augustine, *The City of God* (Books VIII–XVI), Gerald G. Walsh and Grace Monahan, trans., *The Fathers of the Church* series (Washington: Catholic University of America Press, 1952), pp. 249–250, emphasis added.

14. For more information contact Rachel's Vineyard Ministries, 743 Roy Road, King of Prussia, PA 19406, www.rachelsvineyard.org.

Chapter Six: So Now You Are Ready for the Sacrament of Penance

1. Augustine, *Confessions*, bk. 8, chap. 10–11, in Saint Augustine, *Confessions*, Vernon J. Bourke, trans., *The Fathers of the Church* series, vol. 21 (New York: Fathers of the Church, 1953), pp. 221–222.

2. Augustine, *Confessions*, pp. 224–225.

3. *Catechism*, n. 1451, p. 364.

4. Council of Trent, *Decree on the Sacrament of Penance*, chap. 4 "On Contrition," cited in J. Neuner and J. Dupuis, ed., *The Christian Faith in the Doctrinal Documents of the Catholic Church*, revised edition (New York: Alba, 1982), n. 1622, p. 460; see Denzinger and Schönmetzer, n. 1676.

5. *Reconciliatio et Paenitentia*, n. 34; pp. 134–136.

6. Augustine, *The City of God*, bk. 12, chap. 3, in Walsh and Monahan, p. 250.

7. *Code of Canon Law*, canon 978.

8. *Catechism*, n. 1470, p. 369.

9. *Catechism*, n. 1460, p. 367.
10. Rite of Penance, n. 6, in *The Rites of the Catholic Church*, pp. 365–366.
11. Augustine, *The City of God*, bk. 12, chap. 8, in Walsh and Monahan, pp. 258–259.
12. Jerome, "Letter 22: To Eustochium, on the Virgin's Profession," n. 17, in *Select Letters of St. Jerome*, F.A. Wright, trans., *Loeb Classical Library Series* (Cambridge, Mass.: Harvard University Press, 1980), p. 89.

Chapter Seven: The Other Side of the Confessional

1. Alec Guinness, *Blessings in Disguise* (Pleasantville, N.Y.: Akadine, 2001), p. 36.
2. *Reconciliatio et Paenitentia*, n. 29, p. 110.
3. *Code of Canon Law*, canon 986.
4. "A Prisoner's Secretly Taped Sacramental Confession," *Origins: CNS documentary service*, vol. 26, no. 3 (June 6, 1996): pp. 33, 35–36.
5. Lorenzo Albacete, "Secrets of the Confessional," *New York Times Magazine*, May 7, 2000, p. 120.
6. Henri J. M. Nouwen, *The Wounded Healer: Ministry in Contemporary Society* (Garden City, N.Y.: Doubleday, 1972).
7. *Reconciliatio et Paenitentia*, n. 29, p. 110.
8. *Catechism*, n. 1466, p. 368.
9. *Catechism*, n. 1424, pp. 357–358.
10. For the complete story of Marine Chaplain Vince Capodanno, see Rev. Daniel L. Mode, *The Grunt Padre: Father Vincent Robert Capodanno, Vietnam 1966–1967* (Oak Lawn, Ill.: CMJ Marian, 2000).
11. Mode, xvii.
12. Mode, p. 122.
13. Mode, p. 131.

Index

abortion, 106
absolution, 81, 90
   sin and, 120–125
accessibility, 39–40
Act of Contrition, 52, 75–76, 113,
   115–120
Adam, 33
adultery, 35–36
Albacete, Lorenzo, 135
Alcoholics Anonymous, 98–99
Alphonsus Liguori, Saint, 143
Ash Wednesday, 91
Augustine, Saint, 85–86, 93–94,
   95, 106, 123, 127
   baptism of, 118–119

baptism, 75, 91–92
   of Augustine, 118–119
Bartimaeus, 35
Bevins, John, 94
Blessed Isaac. *See* Isaac of Stella
Blessings in Disguise (Guinness),
   131–132
Bonhoeffer, Dietrich, 107–108
Bouyer, Louis, 73–74
Brasseur, Mary Ida, 47
Burke, Theresa, 106

Capodanno, Vincent, 4–5,
   146–149
Cassian, John, 96
Catechism, 30, 38, 47, 75, 87, 95,
   105, 120, 124, 140, 144
Catholicism, 21–22, 26–27
   community and, 79–80

confession in, 1–2
conversion and, 91–93
death and, 82–84
examination of conscience in,
   113–114
excommunication and, 81–82
guilt and, 46–47
humility and, 136
moral theology and, 27–29,
   52, 55
challenges, 138–140
Check, Paul, 97
Christianity, moral theology of,
   61–62
City of God (Augustine), 106, 127
Clinton, Bill, 54
Code of Canon Law, 30
college, 41–42
Confession, 58, 134
   assisting priests in, 49–52
   in Catholic life, 1–2
   ease of, 109–110
   faith and, 78–79
   frequency of, 87–88, 96
   good, 101–104
   meaning of, 144–145
   negative experiences of, 90
   pilgrimages and, 15
   priests and, 36–39, 79, 124,
      136–137
   as punishment, 26–27
   reintroduction of, 14–15
   sacrament of penance and,
      9–10
   sin and, 11